101 Tees

Restyle + Refashion + Revamp

CATHIE FILIAN

An Imprint of Sterling Publishing Co., Inc.
New York

WWW.LARKCRAFTS.COM

EDITOR
Linda Kopp

ART DIRECTOR
Kristi Pfeffer

ILLUSTRATOR
Orrin Lundgren

PHOTOGRAPHER
Steve Mann

COVER DESIGNER
Chris Bryant

Library of Congress Cataloging-in-Publication Data

Filian, Cathie, 1970-
  101 tees : restyle + refashion + revamp / Cathie Filian. -- 1st ed.
     p. cm.
  Includes index.
  ISBN 978-1-60059-822-7 (pb-trade pbk. : alk. paper)
  1. Clothing and dress--Remaking. 2. T-shirts. I. Title. II. Title: One hundred one
tees. III. Title: One hundred and one tees.
  TT550.F55 2011
  746--dc22

                                    2010051469

10 9 8 7 6 5 4 3 2 1

First Edition

Published by Lark Crafts

An Imprint of Sterling Publishing Co., Inc.

387 Park Avenue South, New York, NY 10016

Text © 2011, Cathie Filian
Photography © 2011, Lark Crafts, an Imprint of Sterling Publishing Co., Inc.,
unless otherwise specified
Illustrations © 2011, Lark Crafts, an Imprint of Sterling Publishing Co., Inc.,
unless otherwise specified

Distributed in Canada by Sterling Publishing,
c/o Canadian Manda Group, 165 Dufferin Street
Toronto, Ontario, Canada M6K 3H6

Distributed in the United Kingdom by GMC Distribution Services,
Castle Place, 166 High Street, Lewes, East Sussex, England BN7 1XU

Distributed in Australia by Capricorn Link (Australia) Pty Ltd.,
P.O. Box 704, Windsor, NSW 2756 Australia

If you have questions or comments about this book, please contact:
Lark Crafts

67 Broadway
Asheville, NC 28801
828-253-0467

Manufactured in China

ISBN 13: 978-1-60059-822-7

For information about custom editions, special sales, premium and corporate
purchases, please contact Sterling Special Sales Department at 800-805-5489 or
specialsales@sterlingpub.com.

For information about desk and examination copies available to college and
university professors, requests must be submitted to academic@larkbooks.com.
Our complete policy can be found at www.larkcrafts.com.

CONTENTS

No one article of clothing has such a loyal following as the T-shirt. When you slip on a favorite tee, you have to admit it feels like coming home. It may be the color, a saying, a logo, or the fit—but that shirt is you!

It's hard to imagine that today's T-shirt evolved from the one-piece union suit, a popular undergarment of the 19th century. When miners, farmers, and dockworkers began cutting their union suits in half in the late 1800s to create a T-shaped top and a separate bottom, the tee was born.

Further influences transformed the T-shirt into a fashion staple—from military men fighting wars, farmers harvesting in the heat, and families struggling through the great depression. When movie stars in the 1940s began sporting them, fashion changed forever. And, if you've recently looked at the price on a designer tee, you don't need to be reminded how far they've come up in the world.

This book is all about giving you the potential to create your own designer tees for a fraction of the cost. Every chapter contains at least 10 original ideas, each with a new technique to learn or explore. Many of the tees are so quick and easy to make, you can be wearing one tonight.

It doesn't matter if you're a beginner or more experienced seamstress or crafter. At the beginning of each chapter, you'll find the basic information you need about tools, materials, and techniques to successfully make each project. And, better yet, everything you need to make the tees is easily found at any craft shop or fabric store.

There are plenty of ideas for making tees for yourself, but don't forget they're great gifts. You'll find a special chapter just for the guys, and another for making tees for holidays and special occasions, including tees for moms-to-be.

I love tees as much as you do, and I've had fun creating these designs. Once you feel confident making them, I hope you'll be inspired to create your own. For now, it's time to leave those plain shirts behind. Anyone for tee?

Cathie Filian

I know you want to get started—especially if you have big plans to wear one of your new creations tonight—but before you begin, spend a few moments reviewing these basics for best results.

Types of Tees

Traditionally, tees are made from 100 percent cotton knit fabric, or cotton knits blended with polyester or rayon. They're available in a variety of shapes. The most common tee has short sleeves with a crew neck. Other necklines include scoop neck, V-neck, and boat neck. Sleeves can be anything from long or short to three-quarter length or capped. Tank tops and camisoles made from cotton knits are also in the T-shirt family. The straps on a tank top can be wide or spaghetti style. Baby doll tees or empire-waist tees have a fuller torso that's often gathered.

Where to Find Them

You can find tees at most stores. The styles and colors follow the seasons. If you shop carefully, you can find tees to alter at bargain prices. If you're looking for higher-end cotton tees, don't forget to hit the sale racks at department stores or boutiques.

Repurposing old T-shirts is a great way to revamp your look. Don't forget to shop your wardrobe first. If you can't find what you're looking for in your own closet, try going to thrift shops, yard sales, and clothing swaps.

Getting Started

You don't need much to get started creating your own designs. All you really need to do is choose a design or technique, gather the materials needed, and do a little prep work.

Prepping a Tee

You'll need to launder the tee before you begin. This will remove any sizing from the fabric and preshrink the tee. Don't skip this step! Fabric dye, paints, iron-ons, fusible webbing, transfers, and fabric glue have a hard time sticking to fabric sizing. Always wash the tee in warm water and dry it on medium. Do not use fabric softener or dryer sheets.

Basic Materials

You can embellish a T-shirt with anything from paints and iron-ons to embroidery floss and scrap fabrics. Each chapter in this book features a different technique. At the beginning of the chapter you'll find the items you'll need, as well as basic techniques and tips.

Caring for Your Tee

For most of the projects in this book, machine laundering and drying are fine, but for some designs you might want to hand wash and hang to dry. If you're using iron-ons or fabric paints, refer to the manufacturer's instructions for laundering. For all dyed tees, be sure to wash with like colors.

TEE TIME!

▶

CHAPTER 1

CUT & STITCH

Are you bold enough to go for it? Taking scissors to a perfectly good shirt might seem a bit scary, but slicing and dicing a tee can create some fabulous results. With a few quick snips, you can transform your shirt from a crew neck to a V-neck, or even into a 1980s-inspired off-the-shoulder tee.

BASICS

Necklines and Shoulders

You can create a simple and soft neckline on your tee by simply cutting away the banded or hemmed neck. Be sure to cut as close to the edge as possible. For an even softer look, cut 1 inch (2.5 cm) away from the edge of the band or hem. Of course, you can experiment cutting deeper scooped necklines (if you dare!).

And don't forget an asymmetrical neckline adds interest, as you can see in Royal Strips (page 16). You simply shift the bottom curve of the neckline off center. To arrive at a pleasing proportion for an asymmetrical neckline, you may want to draw the cutting line first using a water-soluble fabric marker. Or, you can make a simple pattern that you can reuse anytime. For a simple V-neck, begin by cutting off the banded or hemmed neckline. Fold the front of the shirt in half lengthwise, and cut at an angle from the center neck to form a symmetrical V.

For more elaborate cuts like an off-the-shoulder or one-shoulder design, as seen on the Ice T-shirt (page 124), you'll want to mark your cutting line first. To do this, slip the tee on a dress form, on a friend, or on yourself. Use straight pins to mark the points on the cutting line, and then use a water-soluble fabric marker to draw the line.

Finishing Touches

One good trait about knit fabric is it doesn't fray, which means you don't have to hem a cut edge if you don't want to. If you decide on a hem, fold the fabric back approximately ½ inch (1.3 cm) and topstitch using a ballpoint needle on your machine and matching thread.

You can also bind the edge with a knit bias tape. To do this, fold the tape over the edge of the fabric and sew through all three layers. Set your stitch to a slightly longer length when working with knits to allow for the stretch.

Strips, Lacing, and Ties

Cut strips from knit fabric or recycled T-shirts at least ½ inch (1.3 cm) wide and as long as desired. Use them to decorate a tee for an overall design. Check out It's Only Rock and Roll (page 16) for inspiration. If you need the strips to look more like cording for laces and ties, grab a cut strip by both ends and gently pull to stretch it and roll the edges. You can see how this looks on Summertime (page 14).

Roses

Everyone loves roses, especially on a lovely T-shirt. Large or small, gathered or rolled, they always add a designer touch.

Gathered Roses

Gathered roses have a delicate wavy edge that is soft and flirty. They look much harder to make than they are. If you practice with scrap fabric first, you'll be whipping out successful roses after only a few tries.

Start with strips cut from old tees or knit fabric. The strips can be almost any size. A longer strip yields a larger flower, and a wider strip yields a fuller flower. For a regular size flower, begin with a strip 1½ inches (3.8 cm) wide and 14 inches (35.6 cm) long. Hand sew or machine stitch a long stitch, called a gathering stitch, along one edge. Don't backstitch or knot the ends. Pull the threads to gather.

Begin rolling one end of the gathered strip toward the other, making three turns as you do. Hand sew the rolls in place. Continue loosely rolling and stitching until you reach the end of the strip. Sew the center of the flower to the tee, then open the petals as you wish and hand tack in place. If desired, you can add a button or rhinestone embellishment at the center of the flower.

Rolled Roses

Rolled roses highlight the texture and layers of fabric. The same principals for determining strip size for gathered roses apply: the strips can be almost any size; a longer strip yields a larger flower; and a wider strip yields a fuller flower. For a regular size flower, begin with a strip that is 2 inches (5 cm) wide and 10 inches (25.4 cm) long. Lay the strip flat. Fold the strip in half widthwise to make a strip that is 1 x 10 inches (2.5 x 25.4 cm). Fold the right end over ½ inch (1.3 cm) to make an angle, and use a needle and thread to hand tack it in place through all layers.

Fold and twist the tail of the strip until it forms a small circle. Working on the back of the circle, hand sew the folds to secure them. Bring the tail to the underside of the completed circle, and continue folding, twisting, and stitching until you've folded the entire strip. Sew the rose to the tee. Add a button or rhinestone embellishment to the center, if desired.

Ruffles

Bring a simple and chic touch to any plain tee by adding ruffles. To make them, first cut a strip of fabric. You can make it as wide as you want, but the length should be two or three times the length of the area where you're attaching the ruffle. Hand sew or machine stitch a gathering stitch along one edge.

Don't backstitch or knot the ends. Pull the threads to gather. For double ruffles, sew a row of gathering stitches close to each edge. For tux ruffles, sew the gathering stitch down the center of the strip.

Pin the ruffle at the desired place on the tee. Take time to adjust the gathers. Spread them out until they are as even as possible, and repin as necessary. Sew along the gathering stitch to attach the ruffle to the tee.

Pleats

Free-form pleats are so simple to make. Begin with a strip of fabric. Pin one end to a starting point, fold the fabric back and forth, and pin. Continue folding and pinning until you reach the end. Sew down the center of the pleated strip, and it's ready to attach to your tee.

Sleeves

Altering or adding sleeves is a fun way to spruce up a T-shirt. You'll find patterns for a bell sleeve, and one for a ruffle sleeve on page 168. Mix and match fabric, patterns, and colors, or go monochromatic for a soft look. Check out Lovely (page 22) and Bell of The Ball (page 23) for design inspiration.

Q & A

Q: *Can I piece fabric strips together?*

A: Yes. Just place the ends with right sides together and sew. If you're gathering the strips, you'll need to stop and restart your gather stitch at the seam. If you don't, you might break your threads when pulling and the gathers won't be even.

Q: *Can I use fabric glue when making roses?*

A: Sure, why not! Add a drop of fabric glue in place of a stitch when making gathered or rolled roses. Allow the glue to dry for each layer before moving to the next. Once the glue is completely dry, simply hand stitch the rose to the tee.

Nothing is cuter on a little girl in the summer sunshine than this fringed tee. A simple overhand knot attaches the strips to the hem.

▶ **1.** Tie-dye a target using purple and light blue fabric dye (pages 56-57). For even more on dyeing, see chapter 3.

2. Use a water-soluble fabric marker to mark small dots around the hem. Place the dots ½ inch (1.3 cm) in from the edge of the hem, and space them 1 inch (2.5 cm) apart. Pierce the dots with the tip of a sharp scissors. Count the number of holes.

3. Cut strips ½ x 12 inches (1.3 x 30.5 cm) from old tees to make the laces. Cut one strip per hole. Pull the ends of the strips for a more corded look (page 11). For this design, I cut hot pink, tangerine, yellow, turquoise, and teal strips to create a rainbow effect.

4. Turn the tee inside out. For each hole, fold the strip in half, thread the loop through the hole, bring the tails through the loop, and pull. Continue until you've knotted all strips through the holes. Trim the ends to make them even or leave them uneven for an even breezier look.

> TIP: You can cut the hemline of the tee to any length. But use an overcast stitch on your machine to reinforce the cut edge before making the holes and knotting the strips.

Alter the bottom of the tee by deconstructing the hemline. Pair the look with gathered roses at the top for a tattered-chic statement that's perfect for a night on the town.

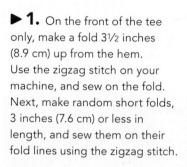

▶ **1.** On the front of the tee only, make a fold 3½ inches (8.9 cm) up from the hem. Use the zigzag stitch on your machine, and sew on the fold. Next, make random short folds, 3 inches (7.6 cm) or less in length, and sew them on their fold lines using the zigzag stitch.

2. Sew around the edges of randomly placed narrow rectangles using the zigzag stitch. With sharp scissors, carefully cut away the inside of each rectangle, leaving only the stitched outline. To complete the look, add a few rows of randomly placed zigzag stitches.

3. Make five gathered roses of different sizes (page 12) from an old tee. Sew them across the neckline. Stitch a mother-of-pearl button at the center of each rose.

Use strips cut from knit fabric or an old tee to accent an asymmetrical neckline. The addition of rolled roses gives this tee soft and sweet highlights.

ROYAL STRIPS

▶ **1.** Cut an asymmetrical neckline from a crew-neck tee (page 11).

2. Cut several strips from knit fabric or old tees, each measuring ¾ x 16 inches (1.9 x 40.6 cm).

3. Attach one strip to the tee all the way around the neckline by stitching down the center of the strip. Join the strips as needed.

4. Pin one end of a strip at the shoulder seam on the narrow side of the neckline. Take the strip over to the other shoulder seam, scooping it as you go to create a pleasing curve, and pin. Attach it to the tee by stitching down the center of the strip. Repeat, using two more strips.

5. Make three rolled roses (page 12). Sew a large mother-of-pearl button to the center of each. Sew the roses to the shoulder seams.

Variation
It's Only Rock and Roll

Go wild! Randomly attach strips to the front of a printed tee. Overlap them in places for more interest. If you don't know what colors to use for the strips, take your cue from the print on the tee.

A narrow line of layered ruffles, gently gathered around the straps on a racer-back tank top, adds a simple embellishment that enhances the shape of the garment.

▶ **1.** Measure around the straps of a tank beginning at one side and ending at the other. Double this measurement.

2. Cut strips of fabric to the length determined in step 1. The strips can be as wide as you wish. For this design, the red strip is 1½ inches (3.8 cm) wide and the tan strip is 1 inch (2.5 cm) wide.

3. Sew a gathering stitch on each strip approximately ¼ to ⅜ inch (6 to 9.5 mm) in from one edge. Pull the threads to gather. Layer the ruffles and pin them around the neckline along the edge of the straps. Adjust the gathers, then sew them to attach them to the tank.

● **Variation**
Bubble Gum

No sewing machine? No problem! Sew your gathering stitch by hand down the center or slightly off-center on the strip. Pull the threads to gather. Lay the ruffle flat, lining up the gathering line with the neckline of a tank top. Hand stitch along the gathering line to attach the ruffle to the tee.

If you're looking for a quick and flirty fix, attach ruffles to the hem of a baby doll tee. Mix and match patterns and prints, or choose a solid color that complements the tee.

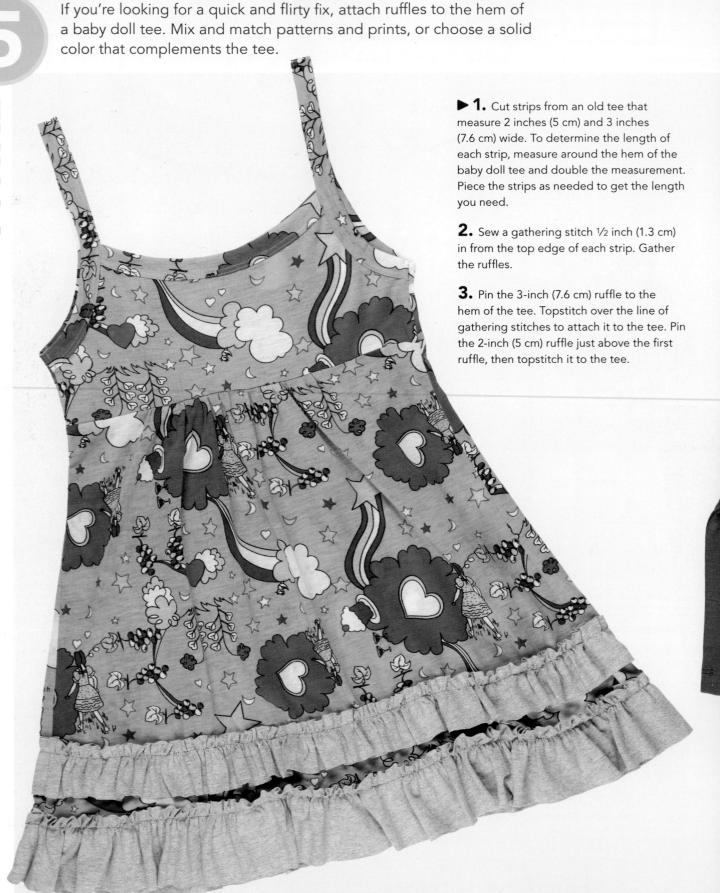

▶ **1.** Cut strips from an old tee that measure 2 inches (5 cm) and 3 inches (7.6 cm) wide. To determine the length of each strip, measure around the hem of the baby doll tee and double the measurement. Piece the strips as needed to get the length you need.

2. Sew a gathering stitch ½ inch (1.3 cm) in from the top edge of each strip. Gather the ruffles.

3. Pin the 3-inch (7.6 cm) ruffle to the hem of the tee. Topstitch over the line of gathering stitches to attach it to the tee. Pin the 2-inch (5 cm) ruffle just above the first ruffle, then topstitch it to the tee.

TWIRL

Variation
Modern Pioneer

No one will believe this sweet neckline ruffle came from a man's old sport tee. To make it, just cut off the bottom of a large tee to make a 3-inch (7.6 cm) strip, keeping the hem intact. Gather the strip ½ inch (1.3 cm) in from the raw edge and set aside. Cut a graceful scoop neckline on the front of a long-sleeve baby doll tee. Pin the ruffle along the cut line, adjust the gathers, and sew. Topstitch a length of gathered sheer ribbon over the ruffle.

Make the ruffle trim for the funky flower by cutting two strips, each ½ x 30 inches (1.3 x 76.2 cm). Gather each strip down the center until each strip measures 15 inches (38.1 cm) in length. Cut a strip 1 x 15 inches (2.5 x 38.1 cm), and sew both gathered strips to it. Curl one end of the strip into a round flower, leaving a short tail for the stem. Pin, and then sew the flower and stem to the ruffle.

PLEATED CLOUDS

6

You can add a bit of sophistication to any tee in no time. Just pleat strips of fabric and attach—it's that simple!

▶ **1.** Cut the neckline of a crew-neck tee into a soft scoop (page 11). Measure the neckline on the front of the shirt from one shoulder seam to the other. Triple that measurement.

2. Cut two strips of knit fabric 1½ inches (3.8 cm) by the measurement determined in step 1. You may need to piece strips together.

3. Pin one edge of the strip to the shoulder seam near the neckline. Begin folding the strip back and forth to create free-form pleats (page 13). Pin and fold as you go along the neckline until you reach the other shoulder seam. Sew down the center of the pleated strip to attach.

4. Repeat with the second strip, placing it just below the first one.

● Variation
Sky Blue

Go off sides to make a bold design. Cut three
strips to make separate pleated embellishments.
Begin by sewing the first pleated strip to the front
of the tee in the upper shoulder area. Add layers
by overlapping the remaining pleated strips.

7

Get all the drama of ruffled sleeves for half the work. Gathered layers highlight one sleeve of this tee for a lovely, fun, and flirtatious touch.

▶ **1.** Copy and enlarge the sleeve patterns on page 168. Cut three sleeves from knit fabric or an old tee. Cut one from the pattern for the large sleeve. Cut two from the pattern for the small sleeve.

2. Sew a gathering stitch across the top of each sleeve approximately ⅜ inch (9.5 mm) in from the edge. Pull the threads to gather.

3. With right sides together, center the large gathered sleeve on the shoulder seam. Place it 2 inches (5 cm) in from the top of the tee's sleeve. Pin, and then sew to attach.

4. In the same way, position, pin, and sew one of the smaller gathered sleeves 1 inch (2.5 cm) in from the first one. Do the same for the last small sleeve, positioning it just under the neckline of the tee.

5. Use the template for the heart on page 170 to cut a fabric appliqué. Sew lines of zigzag stitching of various widths and lengths on the side of the shirt at the hip area. If desired, add words using decorative stitching (page 81). For even more on appliqué, see chapter 4. For more on embroidery, see chapter 5.

Variation
Bell of the Ball

Get your groove on with this belled design. First, cut the sleeves of a long-sleeve tee to three-quarter length. Copy and enlarge the pattern for the bell sleeve on page 168, then cut two pieces for each sleeve. Sew two pieces together at the side seams. Sew a gathering stitch along the top of the bell. Pull the threads to gather. Pin the gathered bell to the end of the cut sleeve, and sew. Repeat for the other sleeve. You can hem the bells to an appropriate length or leave the edges raw. For a finishing touch, stitch a tux ruffle (page 13) along the top of each bell.

Sometimes the style of shirt inspires your design. The wide-banded waist on this tee was just begging for a ruffle.

▶ **1.** Begin with a banded-waist tee. Measure the band on the front of the tee from one side seam to the other. Double or triple this measurement.

2. Working on a double layer of knit fabric, cut two pieces that are as long as the measurement determined in step 1 and 3½ inches (8.9 cm) wide. You may need to piece strips together. **Note:** The band on this shirt is 3½ inches (8.9 cm) wide. Adjust the width of the strip accordingly for the tee you're using.

3. Sew a gathering stitch 1 inch (2.5 cm) in from each edge. Pull the threads to gather. Pin one end of the strip at the side seam, and adjust the gathers across the front to the other side seam. Pin, and then sew along the gathering lines to attach the ruffle to the tee.

Tux ruffles aren't just for prom night! This cute ruffled tee is perfect for any day of the year.

▶ **1.** Cut the neckline of a crew-neck tee into a soft scoop (page 11).

2. Working on a double layer of fabric, cut three strips, each measuring 1 x 12 inches (2.5 x 30.5 cm).

3. Sew a gathering stitch down the center of each strip (page 13). Pull the threads and gather until the ruffles are 5 inches (12.7 cm) long.

4. Center one strip on the neckline on the front of the shirt. Place the remaining strips on either side. Pin, then sew down the center of each ruffle to attach.

CHAPTER 2

PAINTING

Paints, stencils, and silkscreens can transform a tee into a work of art in no time. The tools and materials are easy to find. Any aspiring artist can get fabulous results the first time out.

BASICS

Paint

You can find fabric paint in a variety of colors and forms, including paint pens, brush-on paint, and silkscreen paint. Most craft or fabric stores carry enough colors for painting your own rainbow. It's important to prewash your tees before painting to remove any sizing that might prevent the paint from properly adhering to the fabric. Keep in mind that fabric paint needs to be heat set in order to be washable. Just follow the manufacturer's instructions for the particular paint you're using for best results.

Brush-On Fabric Paint

The beauty of brush-on fabric paint is that you apply it directly to a garment using a paintbrush, foam brush, sponge, or stamp. When dried, it's generally soft and flexible. Use brush-on paint with stencils, foam stamps, and for free-form painting. The paint comes in a variety of finishes, from matte to pearl, from glittery to metallic.

The range of colors is astounding, but if you can't find the color you want, make your own by blending a fabric-paint medium with acrylic paint. Following the rules of the color wheel, you can blend paint colors to create new shades or add a drop or two of white to soften the colors.

Dimensional Fabric Paint

Dimensional fabric paint is thicker than brush-on paint, and is also available in a variety of finishes—shiny, glitter, pearl, matte, and even puffy. Use dimensional paint for lettering, outlining, and adding dimension to any brush-on paint design. Most often, the paint comes in a squeeze bottle with a fine tip. When working with dimensional paints, you should never shake the bottle, which creates air bubbles that could explode on your design. It's common for the tip of the bottle to occasionally clog. If this happens, poke the tip with a long sewing pin or paperclip. For best results, start a bottle on a scrap piece of paper before working on the fabric. If you notice an air bubble in your painted design, pop it with a sewing pin while the paint is still wet. Be sure to heat set the paint, and launder the tee inside out.

Paintbrushes

Always use a brush that is specifically designed for fabric. Fabric paintbrushes are stiffer than most, allowing you to press the paint into the fabric so the paint will cling to the fibers. Use a stencil brush when stenciling. The short, firmly packed, stiff bristles reduce the chances of getting paint under the edge of the stencil.

Foam paintbrushes with wooden handles are great for applying paint to foam stamps and to fruits and vegetables when stamping. You can also use them for stenciling since you can easily control the amount of paint on them. They're inexpensive and can be bought in bulk at most craft stores.

Painting Techniques

The following techniques work well for both beginners and advanced crafters. If you're a beginner, don't let attempting a technique stop you. The more you paint, the bolder you become. As you gain experience, try mixing and matching various painting techniques to create one-of-a-kind designs, or use a silkscreen to create the same image over and over.

Stenciling

For a quick and easy way to paint a tee, try stenciling. You can find stencils that are letters, words, shapes, or all-over designs. When choosing a stencil, think about its size in relation to the tee and where you'll place it on the shirt. The front or back of a tee is a great place for a large stencil, and the upper shoulder or sleeve area is great for a smaller stencil.

Once you know where the stencil will go, secure it to your tee by pressing and holding while you paint, sticking pieces of low-tack tape at the edges of the stencil, or by using a spray of repositionable stencil adhesive on the back of the stencil. If you're working with individual letter stencils, you'll find that lining them up can be a bit tricky. I like to begin by drawing a guide line with a disappearing-ink fabric marker and clear ruler—both can be found with the sewing notions in a craft or fabric shop. I use the ruler to center all the letters on the line and then secure each stencil with low-tack tape.

Once you secure the stencil to the tee, you're ready to paint. To keep the paint from seeping through to the other side of the tee, insert a layer of wax paper inside the shirt between the front and back.

The key to good stencil painting is not using very much paint. It's better to paint two light coats than one heavy coat. I like to squirt a little paint on a pallet, dab the brush into the paint, and tap off any excess paint until the brush is dry. If you overload your brush, the paint might seep under the stencil, creating a sloppy and uneven edge. For best results, paint over the stencil in an up and down fashion, not side to side.

There are many premade stencils on the market. However, if you can't find one you like, you can easily create your own using self-adhesive shelf liner or freezer paper. The freezer paper has a waxed side that adheres to the fabric when you iron it. When you're finished stenciling, simply peel the paper away. The lettering on Moustache (page 33) was made using a black and white copy and some clear shelf liner.

Freehand Painting

Not an artist? Don't worry! Don't let the word freehand throw you. You can still get outstanding results the first time around. For design inspiration, look at clip art, greeting cards, and scrapbook paper. And always remember to use paintbrushes made for fabric painting so the paint will properly adhere to the tee.

Stamping

You can stamp your fabric with anything from traditional foam stamps and household items to fruits and vegetables. You'll find foam stamps come in a variety of shapes and styles and are available at craft and fabric shops. They're often inexpensive. You clean them with soap and water and can use them over and over again. You can also purchase craft foam for making your own stamps.

When painting with foam stamps, pour some fabric paint onto a plastic plate and dip the foam stamp into it (or brush paint directly onto the foam). Then press the stamp onto the tee, and gently lift the stamp to reveal the painted design. Allow the paint to dry before heat setting it according to the manufacturer's instructions. You can layer different paint colors over the stamp for a more colorful design.

I really enjoy stamping and painting with found objects and everyday items. Pencils and hot glue sticks create perfect polka dots, spaghetti creates fine lines, and keys look very cutting edge. It's best to test the stamp first on a paper towel or scrap of fabric because you won't know how the image will look until you pull the item away.

Taped Designs

Use tape when you want to make straight lines, squares, and grids. Painter's tape is low-tack so it doesn't pull the fibers from the tee. Also try using painter's masking for corners to give you a foolproof 90° angle for your designs, as I did on the project Mod Butterflies? (page 36).

When using tape, position it at your desired spot, and then firmly press the edges into the tee. Paint toward the inside of the design using a flat fabric brush and fabric paint. Allow the paint to dry before carefully removing the tape.

Silkscreen

In the past few years, advancements in home silkscreening kits and tools have opened up a world of design possibilities to the crafter. The variety of options and products now on the market makes it

Q & A

Q: Can I mix different brands of fabric paint?

A: I've mixed various brands of fabric paint with great results. If you have any doubts, always test the paint first on a scrap of fabric.

Q: Do I always need to prewash a tee before painting?

A: Yes! Sizing is a combination of starches and stiffeners. If you leave it on your tee, it will interfere with the fabric's ability to absorb the paint.

easier than ever—no more stretching silk or dealing with elaborate photo emulsions. Since each option has its own set of instructions, you'll need to follow the manufacturer's recommendations for best results.

One option is a home silkscreen machine that can quickly turn a paper design into a silkscreen. To defray the cost of the machine, many people purchase it as a group or with a friend. The machine comes with premade designs, but it also allows you to create your own. The best feature about it is your ability to use the designs over and over again. Another option for silkscreening is to buy premade silkscreens that come in kits. You can reuse each screen approximately 20 times. The designs are either all-over motifs or smaller elements that you can cut and paste together.

With either option, you can use a single color of paint, add just a hint of a second color, or make a rainbow blend of colors. For multi-colored designs, use painter's tape to mask off areas between colors. As with all fabric paint, silkscreen paints will need to be heat set. Be sure to follow the instructions provided by the manufacturer.

There's no limit to what you can do with a simple, inexpensive foam stamp. Metallic and dimensional paints add depth and texture to this design.

FLEUR-DE-LIS

▶ **1.** Lay a light-colored tank on a flat work surface. Place a piece of wax paper inside the tank between the front and back to prevent the paint from seeping through.

2. Cover a fleur-de-lis foam stamp with dark green paint. Stamp the image 1 inch (2.5 cm) down from the center of the neckline on the front of the tee.

3. Using a flat, detail paintbrush and metallic green fabric paint, paint highlights on the stamped image. Allow to dry. Next, add a layer of silver metallic paint, and allow to dry.

4. Beginning at the top of the fleur-de-lis, paint small dots of white pearl dimensional paint around the edge of the stamped image.

5. Follow the manufacturer's instructions for heat setting the paint.

Variation
Floral Noir

Repeat a stamped design across the lower front of a tee or close to the hem. Using a single color will give you a monochromatic chic look. If you use more than one color, avoid a messy paint job by letting the paint dry in between stampings. If you want to stamp a partial motif at the edge of the tee, place a large sheet of wax paper under the edge, and stamp half on the tee and half on the wax paper.

Make your own stencils using freezer paper or clear, self-adhesive shelf liner. For ease of cutting, always work on a self-healing mat and use a sharp craft knife. For inspiration, look at clip art or design books.

▶ **1.** Copy the template on page 169. Lay the freezer paper or shelf liner over the template, and tape them together along the edges. Tape both pieces to the self-healing mat. Use the sharp craft knife to cut away the black lines of the design.

2. Use a ruler as a guide to align the stencil on the tee. If you made your stencil from freezer paper, use a warm iron to adhere the waxed side of the paper to the tee. For shelf liner, stick the cutout directly on the tee.

3. Place a piece of wax paper inside the tee between the front and back to prevent the paint from seeping through.

4. Dab a stencil brush in fabric paint. You want to work with a semi-dry brush, so tap off enough excess paint. Working up and down, tap the brush over the stencil.

5. Allow the paint to dry. Peel off the stencil, and follow the manufacturer's instructions for heat setting the paint.

Variation
Moustache

Spell it out! Use letters to illustrate an object or emotion. To make this design, copy the template on page 169, and then follow the instructions for City Rides (left).

1 2

To get the smooth, bold lines on this design, use a flat paintbrush with rounded ends, known as a Filbert. To create depth, layer a deeper shade of metallic paint over a lighter shade of matte paint.

LOVE AND PEACE

▶ **1.** Lay a light-colored tee on a flat work surface. Place a piece of wax paper inside the tee between the front and back to prevent the paint from seeping through.

2. Use tailor's chalk or a pencil to draw a heart in the center of the tee.

3. Paint the inside of the heart using a flat, rounded paintbrush with rounded ends and matte purple fabric paint. Once the paint dries, dry brush a darker shade of metallic purple over the matte purple.

4. Use a narrow, flat paintbrush, to draw a freehand peace sign inside the heart. Paint a border around the heart. Use a ruler or low-tack painter's tape as a guide if needed.

5. Follow the manufacturer's instructions for heat setting the paint.

• Variation
An Apple a Day

To add a quick splash of color to a tee, think paint-by-number. All you need to do is simply paint freehand over an existing motif. Use the design as a guide for choosing colors and brush sizes.

PAINTING

Stamp out a saying, inspiring words, or a name using individual letter stamps. Instead of using fabric ink, use a permanent ink pad, then heat set the ink with an iron.

▶ **1.** Lay a light-colored tee on a flat work surface Place a piece of wax paper inside the tee between the front and back to prevent the ink from seeping through.

2. Working along the neckline, stamp the word giggles with inked letter stamps. Next add the words laughs, dreams, love, and joy in descending order.

3. Allow the ink to dry. Follow the manufacturer's instructions for heat setting the ink.

Channel your inner Warhol. Tape defines the shape for this color-block design. Use bold colors as the perfect backdrop for black, graphic motifs.

MOD BUTTERFLIES

▶ **1.** Lay a tee on a flat work surface. Place a piece of wax paper inside the tee between the front and back to prevent the paint from seeping through.

2. Use painter's tape to mark the outline of one large rectangle or square on a tee.

3. Work one color at a time. Use tape to mark off a rectangle or square inside the larger rectangle or square. Paint the taped-off section with the first color. Allow the paint to dry thoroughly. Continue taping and painting in this way until you've painted all the blocks.

4. Use a foam stamp, silkscreen, or handmade stencil and black paint to stamp, screen, or stencil a graphic motif in the center of each square.

5. Allow the paint to dry thoroughly before peeling off any remaining tape. Follow the manufacturer's instructions for heat setting the paint.

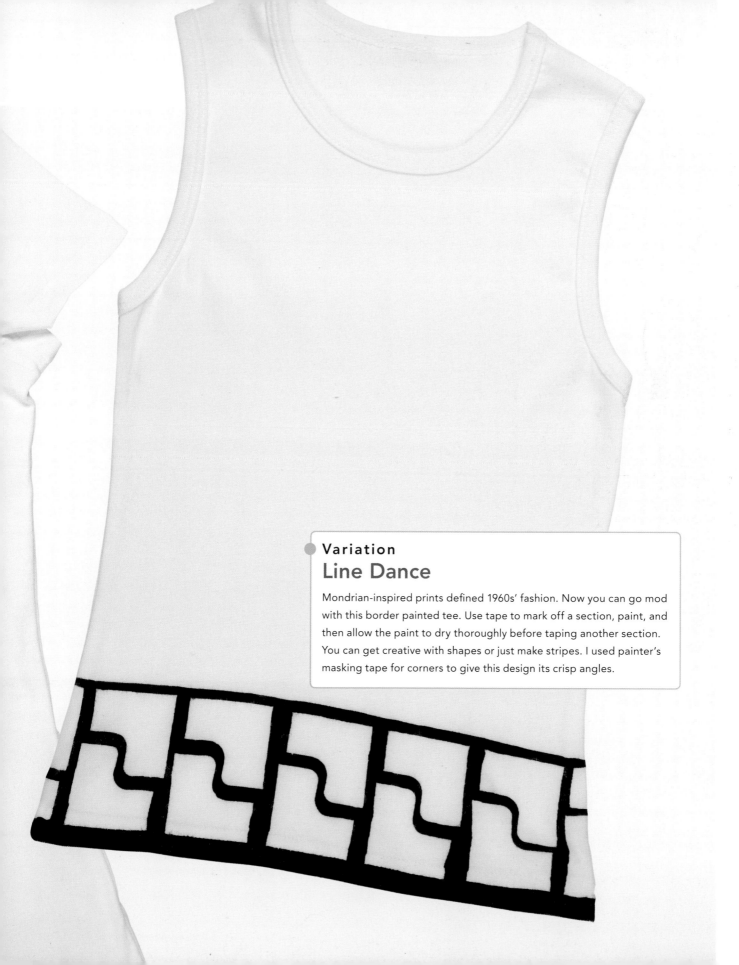

Variation
Line Dance

Mondrian-inspired prints defined 1960s' fashion. Now you can go mod with this border painted tee. Use tape to mark off a section, paint, and then allow the paint to dry thoroughly before taping another section. You can get creative with shapes or just make stripes. I used painter's masking tape for corners to give this design its crisp angles.

It's good to be king! Using one color on a silkscreen design packs a visual impact. No one will deny who's in charge when you wear this shirt.

CROWNED

▶ **1.** Lay a tee on a flat work surface. Place a piece of wax paper inside the tee between the front and back to prevent the paint from seeping through.

2. Position a handmade or store-bought silkscreen (page 29) in the center front of the tee.

3. Apply a long bead of silkscreen paint across the top of the screen. Place your squeegee at a 45° angle, apply an even pressure to it, and then pull a coat of paint down the screen until you've covered the entire design.

4. Lift the screen to reveal your design. Allow the paint to dry. Wash the screen with cold water (don't scrub it), and allow it to air dry.

5. Follow the manufacturer's instructions for heat setting the paint.

Beautiful

Position a screen design off center to make the most of a tee with an unusual neckline.

Beautiful

Variation
Doodled

Try silkscreening over a patterned tee. It's one way to add extra pop to an already cool design.

FLAIR

Make it this afternoon—wear it tonight! Add a little flair to a dressy black tee with silver paint and an art deco-inspired flower stencil.

▶ **1.** Lay the tee on a flat work surface. Place a piece of wax paper inside the tee between the front and back to prevent the paint from seeping through.

2. Position a stencil near the left shoulder of the tee following the neckline. Dab a stencil brush in silver metallic fabric paint. Tap off any excess. Working up and down, tap the brush over the stencil. Don't brush the paint side to side. Allow to dry.

3. Follow the manufacturer's instructions for heat setting the paint.

Throw away the paintbrush for this free-form style of stenciling. You make the random pattern with plastic stencils and watered-down fabric paint in a spray bottle.

BRAZIL

▶ **1.** Lay a tee on a flat work surface. Place a piece of wax paper inside the tee between the front and back to prevent the paint from seeping through.

2. Place a series of large stencils down the side of a tee.

3. Using a clean spray bottle, mix water with the fabric paint until it reaches a consistency that will go through the nozzle.

4. Stand over the tee, and spray the paint over the stencils. **Note:** This is a perfect technique for working outside!

5. Allow the paint to dry. Remove the stencils, and then follow the manufacturer's instructions for heat setting the paint.

PAINTING

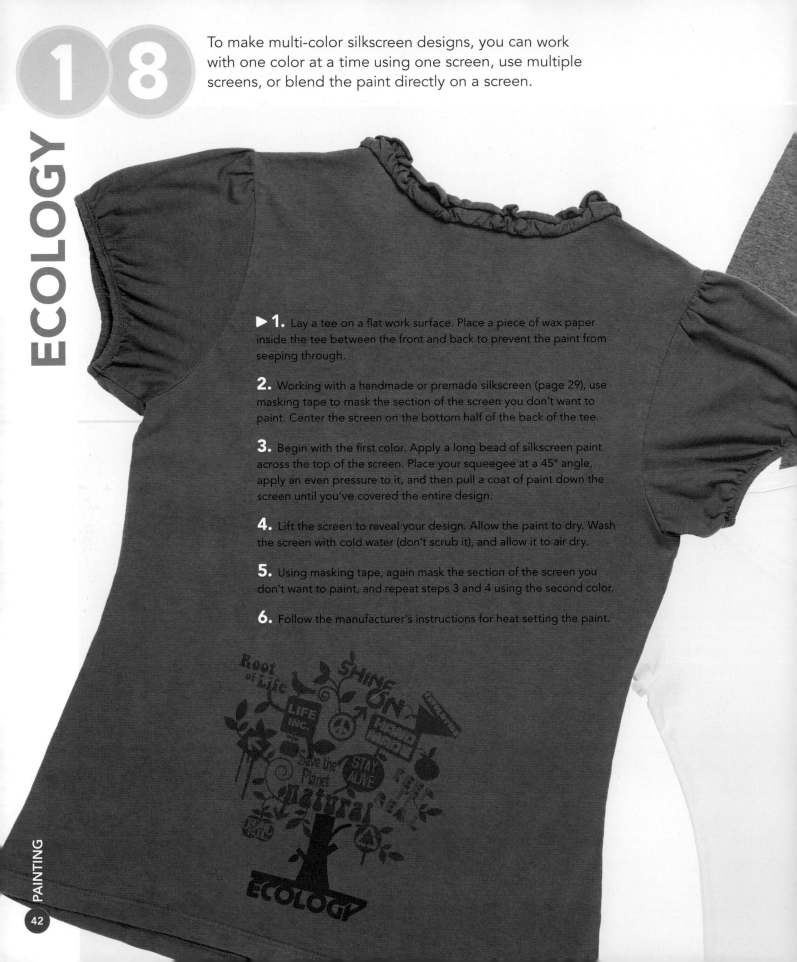

ECOLOGY

To make multi-color silkscreen designs, you can work with one color at a time using one screen, use multiple screens, or blend the paint directly on a screen.

▶ **1.** Lay a tee on a flat work surface. Place a piece of wax paper inside the tee between the front and back to prevent the paint from seeping through.

2. Working with a handmade or premade silkscreen (page 29), use masking tape to mask the section of the screen you don't want to paint. Center the screen on the bottom half of the back of the tee.

3. Begin with the first color. Apply a long bead of silkscreen paint across the top of the screen. Place your squeegee at a 45° angle, apply an even pressure to it, and then pull a coat of paint down the screen until you've covered the entire design.

4. Lift the screen to reveal your design. Allow the paint to dry. Wash the screen with cold water (don't scrub it), and allow it to air dry.

5. Using masking tape, again mask the section of the screen you don't want to paint, and repeat steps 3 and 4 using the second color.

6. Follow the manufacturer's instructions for heat setting the paint.

Variation
Star Power

Mix and match small screens to create an overall pattern on a buttoned tee. Borrow a cue from your paint colors to select bright replacement buttons.

Variation
Pop Life

To make a quick multicolor design, use three different colors of paint. Apply three short beads across the top of the screen before pulling the squeegee down the screen.

Variation
Love

For random touches of color, add a small amount of a different color or colors of paint all over the screen, then let the squeegee blend them together.

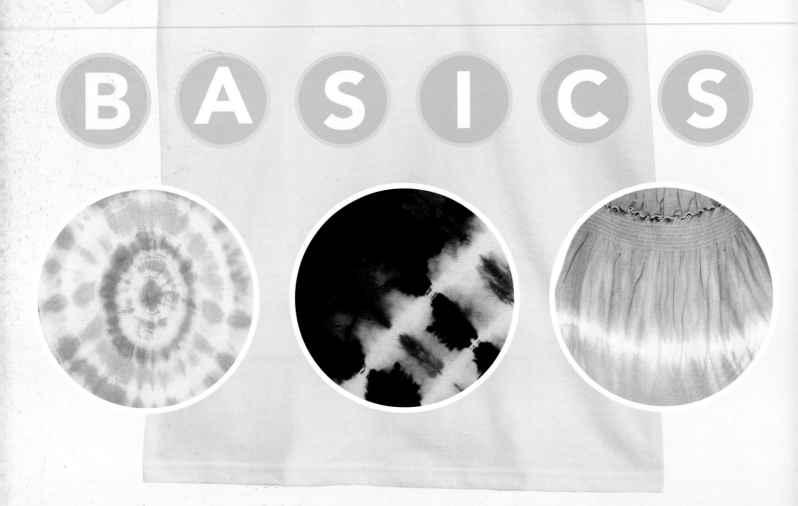

CHAPTER 3

DYEING

You may have heard the old saying, "This is art, not science." And while that holds true for many creative projects, dyeing fabric is both an art and science. Thankfully, the dye companies have perfected the science part, so it's only the art part that you need to worry about.

BASICS

Types of Dyes

You can purchase fabric dyes online, at art supply stores, fabric shops, and craft stores. For the home crafter or beginning dyer, there are only three varieties of dye you need to worry about: fiber-reactive, acid, and all-purpose.

Fiber-reactive dyes are cold water dyes that work best on cellulose fabrics or fabrics made from plants. Fabrics such as cotton, bamboo, linen, hemp, and rayon are cellulose fabrics. Acid dyes are hot water dyes and are perfect for dyeing protein fabrics that come from an animal, such as silk or wool. All-purpose dyes are hot water dyes and have additives so they will dye both cellulose and protein fibers. They are commonly sold at grocery stores in the detergent section.

From Prep to Perfection

You'll need to prepare both the tee and the dye bath before you begin. These few simple steps will guarantee success.

Prepping the Shirt

Before mixing your dye, you'll want to prep the shirt to ensure it receives the dye evenly. Always prewash the shirt to remove any starch and sizing from the fabric's surface, but don't use liquid fabric softener or dryer sheets. **Note:** For best results, use tees made of 100 percent cotton.

Next, evenly wet the tee. You don't want the shirt dripping wet, so wring it out if necessary. I always place my prepared tees in a plastic grocery bag prior to preparing a dye bath. This prevents small dye particles from landing on your wet shirt that can leave unwanted spots.

Step-by-Step Dyeing

Now you're ready for a little color! For best results, be sure to follow the instructions on the dye package. I like to dye in a large glass bowl. Look for bowls that are wide and deep enough to allow the shirt to freely float in the dye bath. You can also dye in a plastic bucket or stainless steel sink. I always wear rubber gloves when dyeing to protect my hands. A wooden spoon is my go-to tool for stirring and mixing dye.

WHAT YOU NEED

Small glass bowl

1 package of dye

4 cups (1 L) of warm water

Large glass bowl

4 teaspoons (20 g) table salt

Rubber gloves

Wooden spoon

WHAT YOU DO

▶ **1.** In the small glass bowl, dissolve the dye in the 4 cups (1 L) of warm water, stirring thoroughly.

2. Fill the large bowl with warm water, leaving enough room to add the dye mixed in step 1. Add the salt, and stir until dissolved.

3. Add the dye mixed in step 1 to the salted water. Place the prepared shirt in the dye bath. Stir for 15 minutes. Soak for 45 minutes or until the desired color is reached.

4. Rinse the shirt in cold water until all the excess dye is removed. A good technique is to place the garment under running water until the water runs clear.

5. Carefully wring the tee or roll it in a rag or old towel to remove any excess water, and hang dry. Wash as usual.

Working with Colors

Fabric dyes allow you to create your own signature shades. You can mix them, brew them strong, or dilute them with water to create thousands of different colors and tones.

All you need to do is follow the principles of the color wheel: red and blue make purple, blue and yellow make green, and red and yellow make orange. To test colors, just dip a white paper towel into the dye bath.

If you want to create a lighter shade of a color, use a smaller amount of dye with the same amount of water. Of course, you still need to add the 4 teaspoons (20 g) of salt. For intense deep color, I use a smaller amount of salted water and keep the T-shirt in the dye bath for the entire 45 minutes.

Making Four (or More) Colors from One Packet of Dye

Using this technique will give you at least four different shades of a color from one dye packet. It's a simple trick and a great way to stretch your dye budget.

WHAT YOU NEED

10 cups (2.4 L) of warm water

1 package of dye

8 teaspoons (40 g) of table salt

2 large glass bowls

1 cup (.25 L) measuring scoop

Rubber gloves

Wooden spoon

WHAT YOU DO

▶ **1.** For the darkest color, mix the 10 cups (2.4 L) of warm water, 4 teaspoons (20 g) of salt, and 1 package of dye in one of the large glass bowls. Stir until dissolved.

2. To create the lightest color, fill the second glass bowl with warm water and dissolve the remaining 4 teaspoons (20 g) of salt in the water. Add a small scoop of dye from the bath mixed in step 1.

3. To create the second lightest color, add a few more scoops of the dye from step 1 to the salted warm water.

4. To make the second darkest color, add more scoops of dye from the bath mixed in step 1 to the salted warm water.

5. Continue either adding dye to the bath or diluting it with warm water to create more colors.

Q & A

Q: *My shirt has decorative trim. Can I still dye it?*

A: Sure! Most trims are polyester; so don't expect it to take the dye 100 percent. Even a slight tint of the color on the trim can look very cool.

Q: *Why do I add salt to the dye?*

A: Salt opens up the pores of the fabric for better absorption of the dye.

Q: *What is the shelf life of mixed dye?*

A: The shelf life of mixed dye is relatively short and depends on the type of dye you use. Most fiber-reactive dyes have a shelf life of four days once mixed. To store mixed dye, funnel into recycled milk or water jugs, and store in a refrigerator or cool dark place.

Q: *What other fabrics dye well?*

A: Beside cotton, linen, silk, nylon, rayon, and wool dye well. Experiment with different fabrics and types of dye for best results.

Dipping and Tying

You don't need to dye the tee one color. Instead of totally submerging the shirt in the dye bath, try dipping a section at a time for a unique look. You can also prepare several dye baths and dip different sections of the tee into different colors. The project Cantaloupe Candy on page 55 is made using this technique.

Tie-dyeing is much easier than it looks. All you need is a few rubber bands and a little bit of tie-dye know-how. In the following projects you'll learn everything from dyeing targets, which you can see on Rainbow Rays (page 56), to stripes, as on Camp Navy (page 53).

Caring for Dyed Garments

You can wash a dyed tee in the washing machine with other clothing without the fear of the color bleeding if you follow a few simple steps. Prior to the first wash, run the shirt under warm water to be sure all the excess dye is removed. Be sure to wash dyed garments in cold water with similar colored items. Remove all items from the washer as soon as the load is finished. Hang to dry or tumble dry.

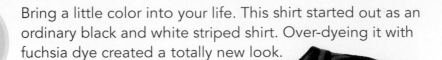

19

Bring a little color into your life. This shirt started out as an ordinary black and white striped shirt. Over-dyeing it with fuchsia dye created a totally new look.

▶ **1.** Wet a prepped black and white striped tee (page 45). Following the dye bath instructions on page 46, prepare a hot pink dye bath.

2. Place the tee into the dye bath and gently stir. Allow the shirt to soak for 45 minutes for deep color. Stir or flip the fabric every five minutes.

3. Rinse the tee, roll it in an old towel to remove the excess water, and hang to dry.

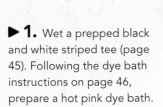

Tie-dyeing an accent at a neckline, wrist, or hem adds new interest to any style of tee. All you need are a few accordion folds, rubber bands, and dye.

MULBERRY

▶ **1.** Wet a prepped V-neck tank (page 45). Following the dye bath instructions on page 46, prepare a burgundy dye bath.

2. Gather the neckline using accordion folds. Start at one side and work toward the other. Secure the gathers with rubber bands, placing them approximately 1 inch (2.5 cm) apart.

3. Dip the banded neckline into the dye bath, and soak until you've reached the desired shade.

4. Use scissors to cut away the rubber bands. Rinse the tank, roll it in an old towel to remove the excess water, and hang to dry.

Dipping just the bottom section of a T-shirt into a dye bath—known as half-dip dyeing—creates a soft design along a border.

I LOVE COFFEE

▶ **1.** Wet a prepped tee (page 45). Decide how wide you want the band of dye to be. Gather the fabric into accordion pleats across the tee at that location. Tightly wrap the section with a rubber band.

2. Following the dye bath instructions on page 46, prepare a brown dye bath. Dip the tee into the dye bath, stopping at the rubber band that holds the gathers.

3. Use scissors to cut away the rubber band. Rinse the T-shirt, roll it in an old towel to remove the excess water, and hang to dry.

LOVE

This double-dip technique works well with either coordinating or complementary color combinations.

► **1.** Wet a prepped tee (page 45). Decide where you want the white stripe. Gather the fabric into accordion pleats across the tee at that location. Tightly wrap the section with a rubber band or two. The more rubber bands you add, the wider the stripe.

2. Following the dye bath instructions on page 46, prepare two dye baths, one teal and one green.

3. Dip the top section of the tee into the prepared teal dye bath. Be careful to stop at the rubber bands. Continue dipping the section into the dye bath until your tee reaches the desired shade. Rinse the top section of the tee.

4. Repeat step 3 for the bottom section, using the green dye bath.

5. Use scissors to cut away the rubber bands. Rinse the T-shirt, roll it in an old towel to remove the excess water, and hang to dry.

OCEAN HOLIDAY

MERLOT

Play ball! For an organic, marbled look, simply scrunch the shirt into a ball and bind it with rubber bands. You'll get a different look each time.

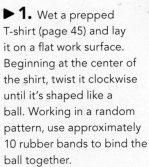 **1.** Wet a prepped T-shirt (page 45) and lay it on a flat work surface. Beginning at the center of the shirt, twist it clockwise until it's shaped like a ball. Working in a random pattern, use approximately 10 rubber bands to bind the ball together.

2. Following the dye bath instructions on page 46, prepare a maroon dye bath. Soak the tee in the prepared dye bath until your shirt reaches the desired color.

3. Remove the balled tee from the bath, rinse, and then use scissors to cut away the rubber bands. Rinse the tee again, roll it in an old towel to remove excess water, and hang to dry.

Dyeing stripes—vertical or horizontal—is one of the easiest tie-dye techniques. Once you've mastered it, you can have fun experimenting with your own designs.

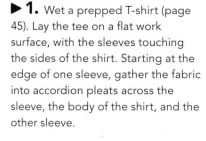

▶ **1.** Wet a prepped T-shirt (page 45). Lay the tee on a flat work surface, with the sleeves touching the sides of the shirt. Starting at the edge of one sleeve, gather the fabric into accordion pleats across the sleeve, the body of the shirt, and the other sleeve.

2. Pinch a section of the shirt together at the center and tightly wrap it with a rubber band or two. Create a second stripe by wrapping a few more rubber bands just below the first one. Continue until stripes of rubber bands encircle the shirt top to bottom.

3. Following the dye bath instructions on page 46, prepare a navy dye bath.

4. Dip the tee into the prepared dye bath, and soak it until it reaches the desired color. Remove it from the bath, rinse it, and then use scissors to cut away the rubber bands.

5. Rinse the tee, roll it in an old towel to remove the excess water, and hang to dry.

● **Variation**
Summer Plum

Stripes don't have to be vertical or horizontal. For this shirt, I pleated and banded just a corner of the tee to create an interesting side highlight.

I loved doodling hearts when I was a teenager—
and I still do. Now, instead of using a pen,
I tie-doodle hearts on T-shirts.

DOODLED HEARTS

▶ **1.** Wet a prepped T-shirt (page 45). Fold it in half lengthwise, matching sleeve to sleeve.

2. Use a water-soluble fabric marker to draw half of a heart shape on one side of the fold. Accordion fold the fabric along the drawn line—you may need to turn it slightly as you pleat to accommodate the curve. Pinch the section together, and tightly wrap one or two rubber bands around the line.

3. Following the dye bath instructions on page 46, prepare a blue dye bath.

4. Dip the tee into the prepared dye bath, and soak it until the tee reaches the desired color. Remove it from the bath, rinse it, and use scissors to cut away the rubber bands.

5. Rinse the tee again, roll it in an old towel to remove the excess water, and hang to dry.

Ombre comes from the French word meaning shadow or shade. This dye technique creates soft graduated colors from dark to light.

▶ **1.** Following the dye bath instructions on page 46, prepare a navy dye bath.

2. Wet a long-sleeve prepped tee (page 45). Use rubber bands to bind off the cuffs and hem.

3. Dip the end of one of the sections in the dye bath, holding it in the dye until it reaches a deep color (approximately three to five minutes). Next, lower the section a bit more into the dye bath, and hold it for a shorter time (approximately two minutes). Then lower the section again, holding it in the dye bath for only a second or two.

4. Rinse the T-shirt, roll it in an old towel to remove excess water, and hang to dry.

Variation
Cantaloupe Candy

Double ombre uses two colors. Each color will go from dark to light and meet in the middle for a soft, blended effect. Following the dye bath instructions on page 46, prepare a peach and fuchsia dye bath. Using the instructions above, dip the top half of the tee in the peach dye bath, then dip the bottom half in the pink. Rinse the T-shirt, roll it in an old towel to remove excess water, and hang to dry.

The target technique of tie-dyeing makes bright and bold designs. Instead of dipping the tee into a dye bath, you use plastic condiment bottles to squirt dye onto the shirt.

RAINBOW RAYS

▶ **1.** Wet a prepped T-shirt (page 45). Lay your shirt on a flat work surface. Decide where you want to place the center of your target. Use your fingers to pinch and pull the center of the target into a cone. Tightly wrap a rubber band around the fabric approximately ½ inch (1.3 cm) from the tip of the cone.

2. Continue adding and wrapping rubber bands down the cone to create the concentric circles of the target; the longer the cone, the bigger the target.

3. Following the dye bath instructions on page 46, prepare six dye baths. **Note:** Since you'll be applying the dye to the shirt and not dipping it, you can make each dye bath in a smaller amount. Use a funnel to pour the dyes into separate bottles.

4. Very carefully, squirt one of the bottled dyes onto the tip of the banded cone. Keep applying the dye until you get the color you want. Rinse the area with cold water.

5. Squirt the next section of the cone with another color of dye. Rinse the area with cold water. Continue this process, using the different colors of dye, until you've dyed each section of the target.

6. Use scissors to cut away the rubber bands. Rinse the tee, roll it in an old towel to remove the excess water, and hang to dry.

Variation
Bubble Gum

Make a two-tone target by rubber banding a cone to make the concentric circles of the target. Then dye the shirt in a pink dye bath. Rinse the shirt, cut away the rubber bands, and rinse again. Next, repeat by rubber banding a cone over the first target and dipping it into a purple dye bath.

Variation
Spring Green

Create moving targets. Place small or large targets on the shoulders, sides, and back of the tee.

Unleash the power of bleach! Un-dyeing uses bleach to remove color exactly where you want it to create your design.

ST. TROPEZ

▶ **1.** Lay the T-shirt on a flat work surface. Place a piece of wax paper inside the tee between the front and back to prevent the bleach from seeping through.

2. Use a bleach pen to squirt a small amount of bleach on a foam stamp. Use a paintbrush to evenly spread the bleach over the stamp.

3. Stamp the design onto the tee. As soon as the color begins to change, rinse the shirt with cold water and a little detergent to deactivate the bleach. Rinse the shirt again, and hang or tumble dry.

4. Once the tee is dry, repeat steps 1 and 2 for as many stampings as you wish.

> TIP: You can also un-dye by drawing freehand on the tee using bleach and a paintbrush. For a more graphic design, try using premade or handmade stencils (page 28). Lay the stencil on the shirt, and apply the bleach in the exposed areas.

Variation
Halloween Sky

Use bleach to create a marbled tee. Begin with a clean, wet shirt, and scrunch it into a ball, as you would do for the project Merlot on page 52. Wrap the ball with approximately 15 randomly placed rubber bands. Soak the balled tee in a bowl of bleach. As soon as the color begins to change, remove the shirt and rinse it under cold running water. To create more elaborate patterns, repeat the process. Rinse the shirt in water and detergent, rinse it again in water, and then hang or tumble dry.

CHAPTER 4

APPLIQUÉ

Appliqués can jazz-up a tee in mere minutes. All you have to do is attach one fabric to another for outstanding results. Whether you hand sew, machine stitch, or use fusible webbing to make your appliqué, let the wide variety of fabrics and lace inspire your designs.

B A S I C S

Sticking to It

I've found that lightweight, paper-backed fusible webbing is a must for making absolutely awesome appliqués. It has two adhesive surfaces, just like double-sided tape, which makes it the perfect material for creating and applying appliqués with ease. You simply iron to fuse your fabric to one side of the webbing, then cut out your motif, remove the paper backing, and iron to fuse the appliqué to the T-shirt. To finish the appliqué, you can stitch or paint around the edges.

Machine Appliqué

You can easily apply an appliqué using your sewing machine. Anything goes when it comes to thread. You can use basic polyester or cotton, or mix it up with silk, shiny, or variegated threads to create a unique edging. Because tees are a knit fabric, use a ballpoint needle in your machine to avoid snags or holes while you sew.

Reverse appliqués give depth to a tee. You machine stitch the appliqué to the wrong side of the fabric, then cut away a piece of the shirt to reveal the motif underneath. You can see how this works on Strawberry Fields on page 66.

Straight Stitch

The straight stitch is the most basic stitch on a sewing machine. Use it to attach an appliqué by sewing around the edges. Hem an appliqué with the straight stitch by turning the edges of the fabric under prior to sewing for a finished look. You can also leave the edges raw and let them fray with laundering for a more artsy look.

Zigzag Stitch

The zigzag stitch adds more texture to an appliquéd project—perfect when you're going for a casual or deconstructed look. Try setting your stitch to various widths for different effects. Just be sure to catch the appliqué on one side of the stitch and the tee's fabric on the other side.

Satin Stitch

This stitch is basically a short, tight zigzag stitch. Use it when you want a beautiful, polished edge on your appliqué. Set the length of your zigzag stitch to the lowest, or almost lowest, setting; the width of the stitch can vary. Make sure the stitch is wide enough to catch the edge of the shirt and at least 1/16 inch (1.6 mm) in from the edge of the appliqué.

Hand-Stitched Appliqué

With hand-stitched appliqué, you can hide your stitches or go for a freer look. I like to use embroidery floss and a ballpoint sewing needle when I want a freehand look. I separate the strands of the floss and only work with two or three at a time. The easiest stitches for freehand appliqué are the running stitch and whipstitch. Look for them in chapter 5, where you'll find a stitch guide on pages 76–77.

Dimensional Fabric Paint Appliqué

Instead of stitching around an appliqué, try using dimensional fabric paint to secure the edges to the tee. You can see how this looks on Flower Pop on page 72. You can find dimensional paint in all colors and in a variety of finishes, such as glitter, glossy, puffy, pearl, and matte.

Lace and Crocheted Appliqués

You can purchase lace and crocheted appliqués from most fabric shops. They're generally available in white, ivory, or black. Beaded lace appliqués always add sparkle. Also try using lace and crocheted collars to enhance a design. Recycled appliqués or collars from old garments are a cost-effective way to repurpose clothing. Look for vintage appliqués at online auctions, yard sales, or thrift shops.

Q & A

Q: *Can I dye lace appliqués?*

A: You can dye cotton or cotton-blend lace appliqués. Just prepare a small dye bath and soak for a few minutes.

Q: *What's better, hand or machine appliqué?*

A: It really depends on the look you're going for. I like hand-stitched for a more homespun, funky look. Machine stitching gives a more polished look, which is great on dressy tees.

Q: *How do I care for appliquéd tees?*

A: If you prewashed the appliqué fabric, you'll have no problems laundering the tee as usual. When pressing, you'll want to use a pressing cloth over appliqués that are metallic, satin, or heat-transferred.

Printed or embroidered fabrics can yield instant appliqués. Just cut out any motifs you fancy, attach them to your shirt with fusible webbing, and then finish them off using stitches on your sewing machine.

▶ **1.** Cut out several motifs from a printed or embroidered fabric. Leave at least a 1-inch (2.5 cm) allowance around the edges.

2. Cut lightweight paper-backed fusible webbing to fit the cutouts. Follow the manufacturer's instructions for fusing the webbing to the wrong side of the fabrics.

3. Cut out the motifs by cutting away most of the allowance you left in step 1. Remove the paper backing, and place the appliqués on the tee in the desired positions. Follow the manufacturer's instructions for fusing the appliqués to the tee. If needed, use a pressing cloth over the motifs.

4. Thread your machine with regular or satin thread, and use the satin stitch (page 62) to sew around the edges.

> **TIP:** Raid your fabric stash to find appliqué ideas. The abstract tropical print on this shirt seemed to pair perfectly with these scraps of embroidered fabric.

Variation
Eclectic Animal

Instead of using a tight satin stitch on the edge of an appliqué, use a long, wide zigzag stitch. For even more texture, stitch random zigzag lines over the appliqués to give the shirt a wild and crazy look.

Combine printed fabric and simple shapes to make your appliquéd design. Hand stitching and buttons add textural interest to this fantastical fabric forest.

CITY FOREST

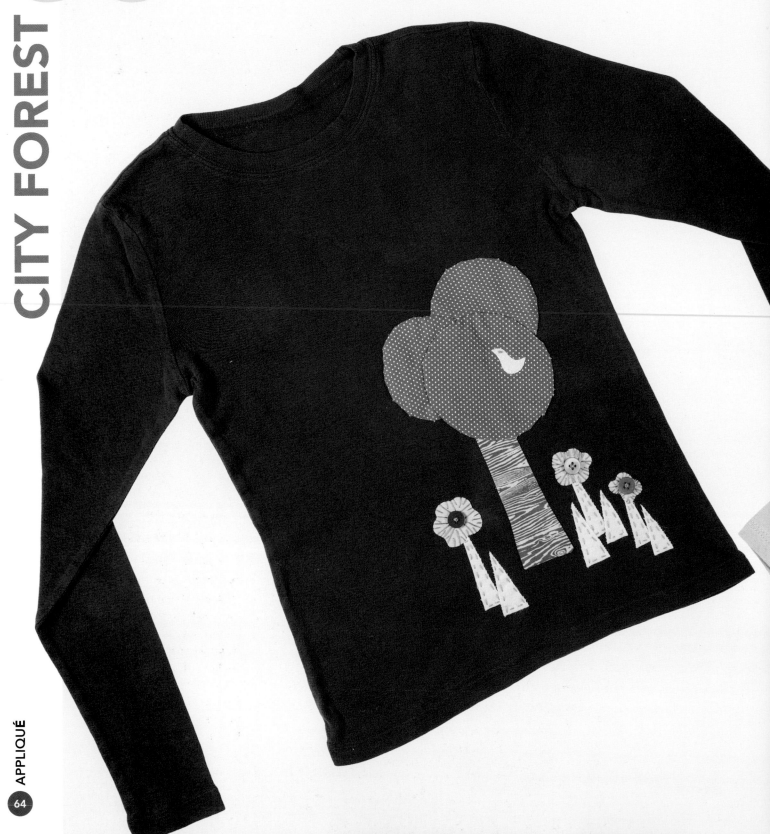

1. Copy the templates for the large tree on page 169. Add a ½-inch (1.3 cm) allowance around the edges, and cut them out. Use them to cut out the fabric: a green for the leaves and a contrasting color for the trunk.

2. For the tree trunk, fold and press the ½-inch (1.3 cm) allowance to the wrong side of the appliqué. Clip the corners if needed to remove any extra bulk.

3. Pin the trunk appliqué to the tee. Use a needle and thread to hand stitch the appliqué to the shirt. Hide the stitches by passing the thread through the fold and taking small stitches along the edge.

4. Repeat steps 2 and 3, using the round appliqués for the leaves. Note: Clip the curves on the circles before you press and fold the edges under to ensure a smooth shape.

5. Copy the templates for the small trees, leaves, and bird on page 169, and cut them out. Apply lightweight, paper-backed fusible webbing to the wrong side of fabric scraps. Lay the cutout templates on the scraps, and cut out the appliqués.

6. Remove the paper backing, and place the appliqués on the tee in the desired positions. Follow the manufacturer's instructions for fusing the appliqué to the tee.

7. Thread an embroidery needle with two strands of embroidery floss. Sew around the edges of the small leaves using a running stitch or a whipstitch (pages 76-77). Embroider a French knot (page 77) for the bird's eye, and attach buttons in the center of the leaves of the small trees.

Variation
Hippie Bird

Go freehand with your stitches to create this little birdie design. Use tie-dyed fabric scraps for the appliqué for a bit of hippie flavor. Flower shapes cut from felt add a crisp, eye-catching contrast to the design. You'll find the templates for the bird and branch on page 168.

Let the print on your tee guide your choice of fabric and shape for reverse appliqués. If you don't have the right colors in your scrap stash, take your tee to the fabric shop and match away!

STRAWBERRY FIELDS

▶ **1.** Select a shape for the appliqué using the print on your tee as a guide. You'll find a template for hearts on page 66, or make your own template for the shape you've selected.

2. Cut out your template and use it as a guide to cut the shape from a solid color fabric. Leave at least a 1-inch (2.5 cm) allowance around the edges.

3. Turn the T-shirt inside out. Position the shape right side down on the front of the tee, and pin it in place.

4. Sew through both layers, approximately ¼ inch (6 mm) in from the edge of each appliqué.

5. Turn the T-shirt right side out. Approximately ¼ to ½ inch (6 mm to 1.3 cm) in from the stitching line, cut away the knit fabric to reveal the appliqué underneath.

> TIP: You don't have to limit yourself to one appliqué per shirt—sometimes the more the merrier.

If you love that old shirt, give it a new life. Cut out motifs from a beloved old tee to make your reverse appliqués.

▶ **1.** Cut a motif from an old T-shirt. Leave at least a 1-inch (2.5 cm) allowance around the edges.

2. Turn the T-shirt inside out. Position the motif right side down on the front of the tee, and pin it in place.

3. Sew through both layers, approximately ¼ inch (6 mm) in from the edge of the appliqué.

4. Turn the T-shirt right side out. Approximately ¼ to ½ inch (6 mm to 1.3 cm) in from the stitching line, cut away the knit fabric to reveal the appliqué underneath.

> **TIP:** Add buttons, rhinestones, or decorative stitches to enhance any design.

Variation
Midnight Mermaids

I love these stylized mermaids! Repurposing them meant I could have them in my life a little bit longer. Using multiple motifs for appliqués is a simple way to create a larger design on a T-shirt. I added rhinestones to my little friends for extra sparkle.

INNOCENT

A reverse appliqué of lace on the shoulders gives an otherwise plain tee a soft, romantic look. I used a V-neck T-shirt for this project, but you can easily adapt it for any scoop-neck tee or tank.

▶ **1.** Make a yolk pattern from the shirt. Place a piece of tracing paper over the top front of the shirt. Use a pencil to draw around the neckline, along the shoulder and sleeve seams, then across the front of the shirt.

2. Transfer the tracing to craft paper, and add a ½-inch (1.3 cm) seam allowance around the edges. Cut out your pattern.

3. Use the pattern to cut a yolk from lace fabric. **Note:** Since a V-neck divides the yoke, be sure to cut a piece for each side.

4. Turn the T-shirt inside out. Position the lace yoke right side down on the front of the tee, and pin it in place.

5. Sew through both layers along the neckline, on the shoulder and sleeve seams, and across the bottom of the yolk.

6. Turn the T-shirt right side out. Cut away the knit fabric to reveal the lace underneath.

7. If you're using a V-neck shirt, add extra detail by sewing a small pearl button at the center of the V.

> TIP: Avoid embarrassing situations by being careful where you place the lace! The yoke, hip area, top center back, and sleeves are all good places for lace reverse appliqués.

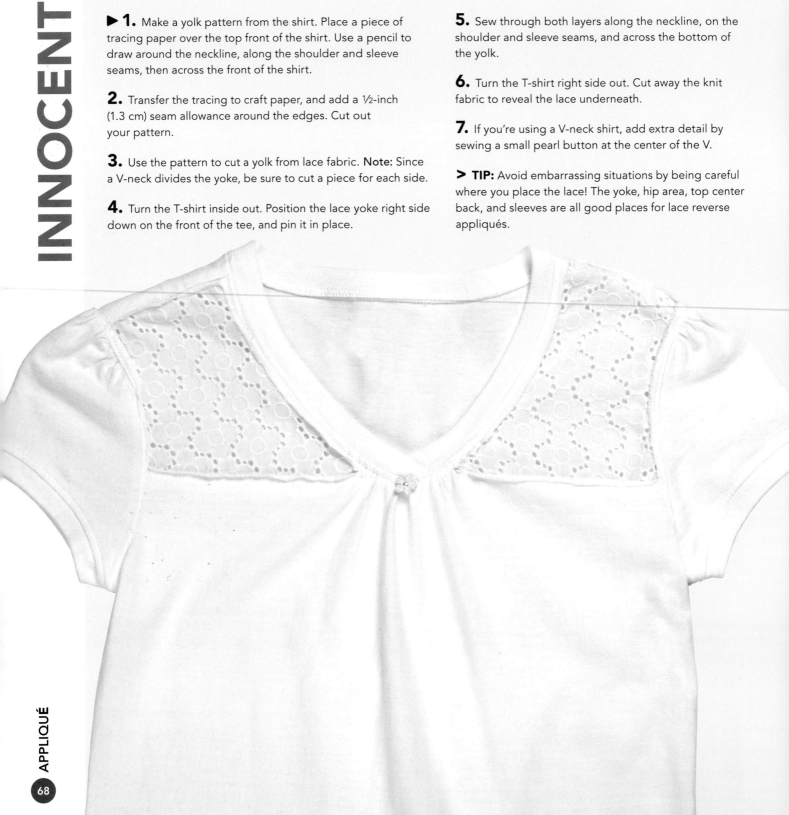

APPLIQUÉ

When looking at beautiful beaded white-lace appliqués in fabric shops, I used to think only of silk gowns and candlelit weddings. Now I think of all the chic tees I can make with them!

ASPEN

▶ **1.** Position a lace appliqué on your tee at the desired location—for this design, I chose to skirt the neckline on the upper yoke.

2. Use either fabric glue or hand stitches to secure the appliqué to the tee.

Crocheted doilies are anything but stodgy. For this design, I first dyed the doily purple to match the tee.

PLUM PUDDING

▶ **1.** Use a V-neck tee and a round, 9-inch (22.9 cm) crocheted doily. Fold one-third of the doily back toward the center so it partially overlaps itself. Pin the doily to the tee along the fold line, placing it around the neckline just above the sleeve. Hand or machine stitch the doily to the tee.

2. Lay a length of velvet ribbon half on the doily and half on the tee. Stitch the ribbon to the shirt, and then stitch a line of small beads on the ribbon.

● **Variation**
Not Your Granny's Square

Sew multiple crocheted squares or rounds to the front of a baby doll tee. You can find premade squares at craft or fabric shops, or, if you're handy with a crochet hook, make your own.

Alter the neckline of a scoop-neck tee using a lace collar for an almost instant transformation. Look for collars at fabric and specialty costume shops, or simply recycle one from an old or vintage garment.

▶ **1.** Lay the collar on the shirt. Don't be concerned with matching the collar to the neckline. Allow the natural curve of the collar to lie on the tee. The curve of the collar will become the new neckline.

2. Use fabric glue to tack the collar to the tee. Once the glue is dry, sew the collar by hand to attach it.

3. Remove the original neckline of the tee by cutting the fabric away as close to the collar as possible.

FLOWER POP

Dimensional fabric paint offers a quick, no-sew alternative to finishing the raw edges of a fabric appliqué. Leave the paint puffy, or use a paintbrush to feather it flat.

▶ **1.** Cut out a floral motif from a printed fabric. Leave at least a 1-inch (2.5 cm) allowance around the edges.

2. Cut lightweight, paper-backed fusible webbing to fit the cutout. Follow the manufacturer's instructions for fusing the webbing to the wrong side of the fabric.

3. Cut out the motif by cutting away the allowance you left in step 1. Remove the paper backing, and place the appliqué on the tee in the desired position. Follow the manufacturer's instructions for fusing the appliqué to the tee.

4. Slide a piece of cardboard inside the tee to prevent the paint from seeping through. Use glitter dimensional fabric paint in a coordinating color to paint around the edges of the appliqué. If desired, use your paintbrush to feather the paint onto the tee.

5. Allow the paint to dry overnight. To care for the shirt, launder it inside out, and use a pressing cloth when ironing.

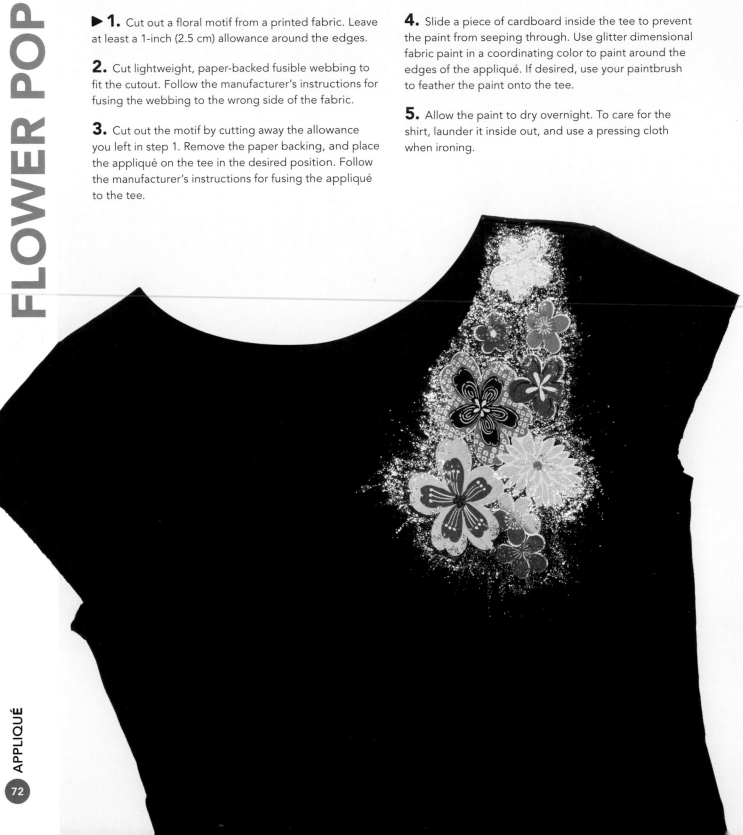

For reverse appliqué, you cut away a piece of the shirt to reveal the sewn motif underneath. With washings, the raw edge of the knit material rolls away from the appliqué for a deconstructed look.

▶ **1.** Cut a motif from a cotton print. Leave at least a 1-inch (2.5 cm) allowance around the edges.

2. Turn the T-shirt inside out. Position the motif right side down on the front of the tee, and pin it in place.

3. Sew through both layers, approximately ¼ inch (6 mm) in from the edge of the appliqué.

4. Turn the T-shirt right side out. Approximately ¼ to ½ inch (6 mm to 1.3 cm) in from the stitching line, cut away the knit fabric to reveal the appliqué underneath.

5. You can add extra detail by gathering the fabric removed from the tee into a flower shape. Sew the fabric flower to the top shoulder of the tee. Cover a button in matching fabric used for the appliqué, and then sew the button to the center of the flower.

> TIP: Have a favorite tee with a bad stain? This technique gives new life to any shirt you just can't do without.

CHAPTER 5

EMBROIDERY

Adorning your tees with embroidery using yarn, thread, or embroidery floss always gives you outstanding results. Knowing a few basic stitches provides almost unlimited design potential. So pick up that needle and thread—you don't need years of experience to expertly embellish that tee.

BASICS

Hand Embroidery Tools and Materials

Needle, floss or thread, an embroidery hoop—you'll only need a few basic tools and materials. They're inexpensive, and you can find them at most craft or fabric stores.

Embroidery Floss

Skeins of floss are color-coded by number, but I prefer to call all the colors by name. If you see a design you like, but are not fond of the colors I used, feel free to use whatever colors you want.

Floss generally comes in six-strand skeins. For each project using embroidery floss, I will tell you how many strands to use. Sometimes you may use all six strands as one.

Embroidery Needles

When you look at an embroidery needle, you'll notice it has a larger eye than a regular sewing needle to accommodate the thicker floss. It's always best to purchase a value pack with multiple sizes. Also consider buying an inexpensive, rubber needle puller. They help you fight finger fatigue and make embroidering a breeze.

Embroidery Hoop

The hoop holds the fabric taut to make stitching easier. You're able to move the hoop to each new area of stitching as you work. I've found wooden hoops tend to snag knit fabric and prefer using plastic ones when embroidering tees.

Transfer Materials

Transferring an embroidery pattern to your tee is easy when you use either a pencil, embroidery transfer paper, or a water-soluble fabric marker. If you purchase an embroidery design, follow the manufacturer's instructions for transferring it to your fabric.

When lettering, use a sharp pencil; the pencil marks will come out in the wash. Transfer paper works best on both simple and detailed designs. Use a water-soluble fabric marker for drawing a design freehand. When you follow the manufacturer's instructions for the transfer paper or marker, the lines will disappear once your job is done.

Let's Get Stitching

You'll use a few basic stitches for all the designs in this book. Once you become comfortable making them, I encourage you to experiment with new stitches and freehand stitching to create your own designs and patterns.

Straight Stitch or Running Stitch

The stitches can be long or short. A series of straight stitches is called a running stitch.

Backstitch

This stitch creates a solid line of stitches that is perfect for outlining designs.

Split Stitch

After you make the first stitch, bring the needle up through the middle of the first stitch to split it. Then continue splitting the stitches as you follow your line of embroidery.

Chain Stitch

This stitch creates a small loop. Use it to stitch a line, or work it in a circle to make a flower. Some of you might know it as the lazy daisy stitch.

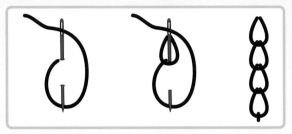

Satin Stitch

Parallel rows of straight stitches made in satin stitch will fill in an outline.

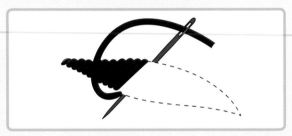

Blanket Stitch

Use the blanket stitch when you want to accentuate an edge.

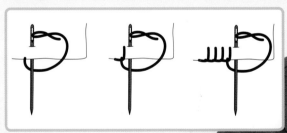

French Knot

Add texture and interest with this elegant little knot.

Whipstitch

Also called the overcast stitch, the whipstitch is used to bind edges. It's perfect for finishing appliqués.

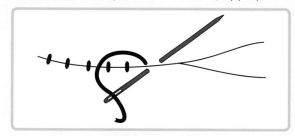

Freehand Stitching

With freehand stitching, anything goes. Try stitching a series of crisscross straight stitches to create little stars, make loops for flowers, or knot the floss as you stitch for polka dots.

Machine Embroidery

Many basic sewing machines come equipped with patterned or alphabet stitches to use when machine embroidering. The stitches can vary from a simple zigzag to ornate scrolls. You can use the alphabet stitches to write a saying or to personalize a tee with a name or monogram.

Always use a non-woven stabilizer on the wrong side of the fabric when machine embroidering on knits. It supports the fabric and prevents it from stretching. When you finish your embroidery, you simply tear the stabilizer away.

If you want to take machine embroidery to another level, consider purchasing a special, computerized embroidery sewing machine. It uses premade templates or allows you to make your own custom designs. There are different brands on the market, and you can find them at any shop that sells sewing machines.

Creating classic, stylish edging is easy with the blanket stitch. Use it anytime you want to add a perfect decorative touch to your tee.

BAJA, CALIFORNIA

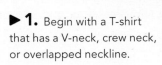

▶ **1.** Begin with a T-shirt that has a V-neck, crew neck, or overlapped neckline.

2. Thread an embroidery needle with six strands of embroidery floss. Use a color that is darker or lighter than the tee color for the best contrast. Work the blanket stitch (page 76) over the knit ribbing on the neckline.

3. Thread an embroidery needle with three strands of floss in a complementary color. Add a row of straight stitches in a V pattern on the ribbing.

Variation
Hibiscus

Embroidered edging isn't just for necklines. Hemlines and sleeves are perfect places to add a little decorative stitching.

Embroider the chain stitch along the neckline of a tee or tank and you won't need to wear a necklace. For extra bling, mix in a few strands of metallic floss with the regular floss.

LOCK AND KEY

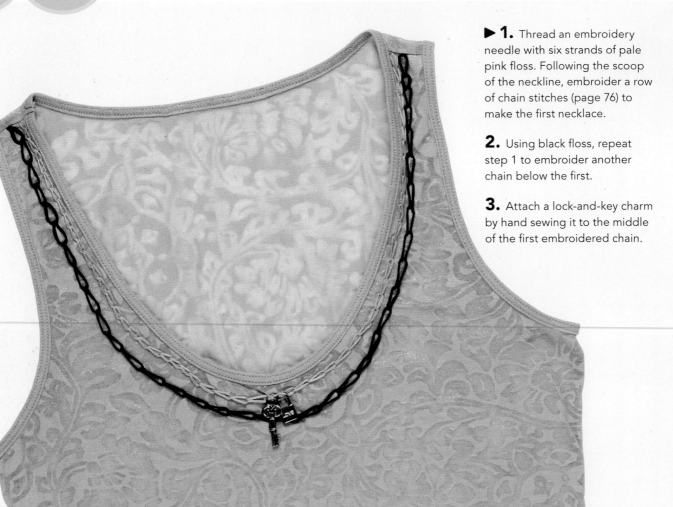

▶ **1.** Thread an embroidery needle with six strands of pale pink floss. Following the scoop of the neckline, embroider a row of chain stitches (page 76) to make the first necklace.

2. Using black floss, repeat step 1 to embroider another chain below the first.

3. Attach a lock-and-key charm by hand sewing it to the middle of the first embroidered chain.

Spell it out! Embroidered words on a tee let the world know exactly what you're feeling. Draw the letters freehand, or make a simple template using your computer.

▶ **1.** Use a water-soluble fabric marker to write the word Bliss in cursive along the side of the neckline. You can also use the template on page 170 as a guide.

2. Place the shirt in an embroidery hoop. Thread an embroidery needle with six strands of white embroidery floss. Embroider the letters using the backstitch (page 76).

> TIP: To make a template using your computer, type in the word or words, adjust the font to your liking, and print it out. Use the template as a reference when drawing the letters, or place transfer paper underneath to transfer the word to the fabric.

With freehand embroidery you just go with the flow, allowing the style of shirt to lead you. Pockets, shoulder straps, necklines, and hems are all great places to add a few stitches.

ENSENADA

▶ **1.** For this design, I used a mix of floss colors and stitches on a smocked, baby doll tank. For each color, I threaded an embroidery needle with six strands of floss. I began with red floss to work the whipstitch (page 77) around the edges of the straps.

2. Then I used a variety of colors of floss to whipstitch over the elastic threads in the smocked bodice.

3. On the pockets, I added a running stitch (page 76) in yellow across the top. Next, I stitched a series of Xs in navy. Then I added a row of chain stitches (page 76) across the pocket in orange.

4. To finish, I worked the blanket stitch (page 76) in yellow across the hem, along with a line of small running stitches (page 76) in orange.

Embellish your tee with a variety of stitches, colors, and shapes. Use a water-soluble fabric marker to draw your designs, then add felt appliqués, buttons, or gems as desired.

► **1.** Use the templates on page 170 as your guide. Work on the back of a plain T-shirt. For this design, I embroidered with peach, raspberry, and light blue floss.

2. Use a water-soluble fabric marker to draw a peace sign, and then embroider it with the split stitch (page 76) using six strands of peach floss. Make the lines bolder by stitching a second row next to the first. Highlight the peace sign by embroidering a running stitch (page 76) around it. Use the same color of floss to stitch a few Xs at the neckline.

3. Draw a heart near the peace sign using a water-soluble fabric marker. Embroider the heart with the backstitch (page 76) using six strands of raspberry floss.

4. Cut a small flower from felt, and position it near the peace sign and heart. Thread an embroidery needle with two strands of light blue floss. Attach the flower to the tee using the running stitch around the outer edge. Add some freehand stitches to the center of the flower using the same color of floss.

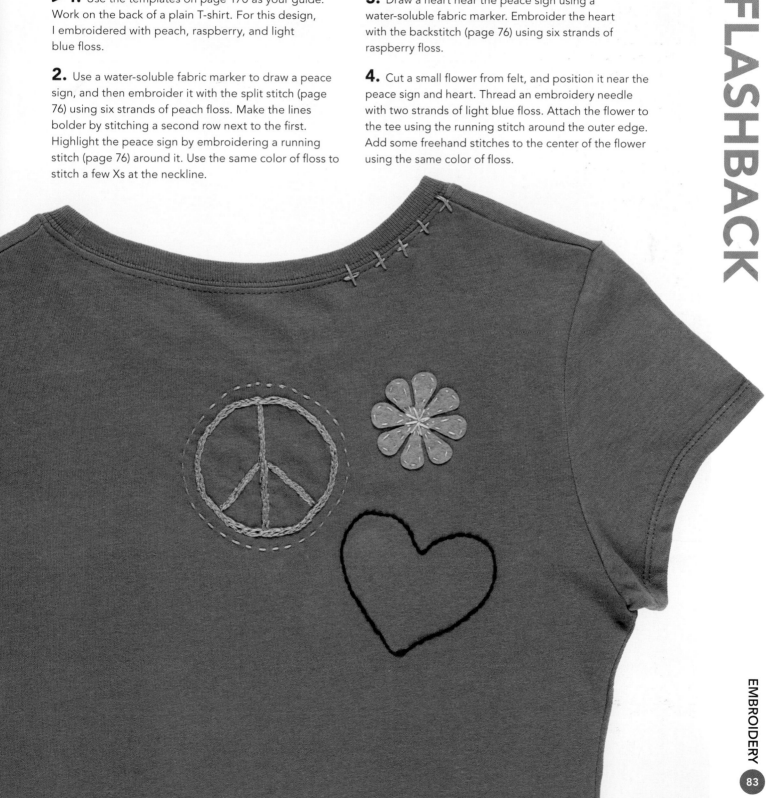

Fill in or enhance a silkscreen design on a tee with embroidery. Think of it as coloring with thread!

PIÑA COLADA

▶ **1.** Use a tee with a silkscreen print or a tee that you've silkscreened (page 29) with your own design.

2. Use the split stitch (page 76), straight stitch (page 76), or satin stitch (page 76) in colors of your choice to fill in or highlight the silkscreened design.

EMBROIDERY

Variation
Gleefully Sing

If you want to alter band or show concert T-shirts, consider this quick fix. Start with a tee screened with a music-themed design, then highlight select areas with embroidery. There's no right or wrong way—just go for it!

If you've never used embroidery transfer paper, try it out on this sweet motif. Look for embroidery patterns online, in books, in fabric shops, or sketch your own.

LITTLE DEER

▶ **1.** Following the manufacturer's instructions, copy the motif on page 171 onto embroidery transfer paper. Transfer the image to the tee.

2. Thread an embroidery needle with six strands of dark gray floss. Embroider the outline of the deer using the backstitch (page 76). Then use the satin stitch (page 76) to fill in the hooves, nose, and eyeball.

3. Using four strands of light gray floss, embroider the backstitch or the split stitch (page 76) for the shading.

Add the right grace note to a plain neckline with a touch of machine embroidery. Use darker thread on a light tee, and lighter thread on a dark tee for the best color contrast.

▶ **1.** Cut a strip from non-woven stabilizer (page 77) that is the length of the front of the neckline. Place the strip on the wrong side of the fabric just below the neckline.

2. Set your machine for a decorative stitch. Make sure you're using the correct presser foot.

3. Line the presser foot up with the banding on the neckline. Stitch along the neckline. Tear the strip of stabilizer away from the stitching when you're finished.

FOXY

This design uses an embroidery sewing machine for stitching this little vixen on the tee. If you don't have one—and are captivated by machine embroidery—you may want to investigate this nifty tool.

▶ **1.** Copy the pattern on page 170. Upload the design to the machine. Place a layer of non-woven stabilizer under the front of the tee where you wish to place the motif.

2. Using the machine's placement guide as a reference, position the tee in the machine's embroidery hoop and attach it to the machine.

3. Following the manufacturer's instructions, set the machine and begin stitching.

4. When finished, remove the tee from the hoop. Trim all the threads, and tear away any excess non-woven stabilizer.

Tiny details can have a big impact.
Use the print on a T-shirt to
inspire your embroidery.

48

CHERRY

▶ 1. Use a water-soluble fabric marker to draw the design freehand on the shirt at the desired location. You'll find a template for the cherries used here on page 170.

2. Thread an embroidery needle with six strands of red floss. Use a satin stitch (page 76) to embroider the cherries.

3. Use four strands of black floss to embroider lines of backstitching (page 76) for the stems.

4. Complete the motif by using four strands of green floss to backstitch the outline of the leaves.

> TIP: You can also trace a motif from the print on your tee, and then transfer it to the fabric for embroidering.

CHAPTER 6

RIBBONS & TRIM

Any ho-hum tee will become a boutique-worthy beauty with the addition of ribbons and trim. A dash of satin, a bit of lace, or an incredible button or two can add fun and flair. Use up your scraps, or go on a treasure hunt for just the right notion.

BASICS

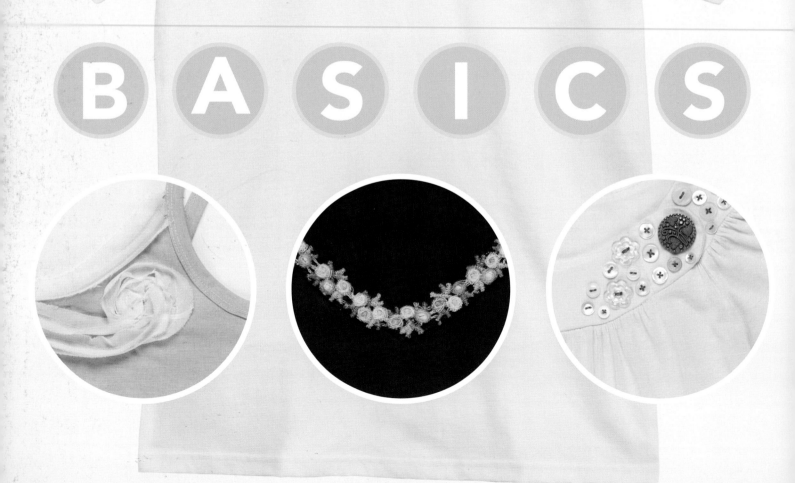

Ribbons

Ribbons come in many finishes that will add a variety of textures to your tee. Whether grosgrain, velvet, or satin, you'll find ribbons in a wide array of prints and colors, including those with seasonal themes, stripes, and polka dots.

You can also make your own ribbons by cutting strips from fabric. For a frayed look, pull the threads along the edges. For a fun look, cut the edges with pinking shears or other decorative-edge scissors, or use your machine to zigzag the edges.

Grosgrain

Its tiny ribbing is the signature of this durable ribbon. Grosgrain is a great choice for decorating T-shirts because it washes well and looks crisp even though it's soft and flexible.

Velvet

Treat these plush ribbons with a little extra care and they'll remain just as beautiful as they were when you first sewed them to your tee. Avoid any treatment that will flatten the velvet or make it shiny. When you iron a shirt with velvet ribbon, be sure to use a pressing cloth.

Satin

Satin ribbons make beautiful bows with long flowing tails. The ribbon may be single-face, which is shiny on one side and dull on the other, or double-face, which is shiny on both sides.

Organza Ribbon

Sheer in appearance, organza ribbons tend to sparkle when the light catches them. Use them to highlight a date-night tee.

Trims

Trims are in! The sky's the limit when it comes to choosing them: from ruffled lace to rickrack to crocheted patterns. Look for trims that are lightweight, soft, and flexible to avoid that scratchy feeling on your skin.

A: Yes, absolutely! Start with a pale shade of cotton or silk ribbon for best results. Cotton laces also dye extremely well.

Q: What about buttons?

A: Believe it or not, yes you can. Just soak plastic buttons in a prepared dye bath for a few minutes.

Ruffled Lace

Look for single- or double-ruffled lace. Single-ruffled lace is gathered along one side, creating one ruffled edge. Double-ruffled lace is gathered down the center, creating two edges with ruffles.

Rickrack

You can't mistake this zigzag trim for any other. Rickrack is sold in packages and by the yard at most fabric stores.

Decorative Trim

You know it when you see it. Usually it features a string of embroidered flowers or is made from braided or woven threads. It's perfect for edging around a neckline or sleeve.

Crochet and Knit Trims

If you're handy with a knitting needle or crochet hook, make your own. Otherwise, buy them ready to go by the yard. Many of the patterns are floral or lacy. Most of them are soft, making them especially suited for decorating a neckline.

Buttons

Buttons are available in so many shapes and sizes that most fabric stores feature a whole aisle of them. You can find seasonal, rhinestone, retro, and kid-themed buttons to match just about any design.

You can use shank or sew-through buttons to embellish your tee. Shank buttons generally lie a little higher on the fabric than sew-through buttons, creating a more dimensional look. If you want to jazz-up a plain sew-through button, try sewing it on using a contrasting color of thread. Don't forget that you can also cover buttons with any fabric for a custom look. You'll find kits for making them at any fabric shop.

Flowers

Silk flowers add instant, flirty fun to any tee. If you want to add a bit of sparkle to the flowers, sew a button in the center, or glue a few rhinestones to the petals. Even though we call them silk flowers most of them are made from polyester fabric, which allows you to wash them with ease. However, for best results, I suggest hand washing shirts embellished with silk flowers.

Attaching Ribbons and Trim

You can attach ribbons and trims to a T-shirt by either sewing or gluing them on. Whether you're hand or machine stitching, use a ballpoint needle to prevent snagging the knit fabric. There are many different fabric glues on the market. Look for glue that dries soft and crystal clear, is washable, and bonds to fabric, leather, lace, and trim.

I fell in love with these bold pink buttons, and immediately thought of rickrack for making their stems. It turned out to be the perfect choice for this child's baby doll tee.

▶ **1.** Cut rickrack into three different lengths. For this design, I used two different colors of green. Stitch the rickrack to the tee to create long vertical stems.

2. Cut leaf shapes from green felt. Sew the leaves to the tops of the stems. Sew the buttons on top of the leaves.

> TIP: If you want to highlight a detail on the shirt, add an extra embellishment of ribbon in a color that matches the buttons.

This is a great project for using up those little scraps of ribbon that haunt your craft bins. For added texture, use ribbon that features a pattern, such as this polka-dot grosgrain.

▶ **1.** Position short pieces of ribbon in a crisscross, overlapped pattern just below the ribbed neckline of your T-shirt. Use a small dab of fabric glue to hold them in place.

2. Machine stitch around the edges of each ribbon using a ballpoint needle.

3. Use small, detail scissors to cut away the neckline of the tee, cutting as close to the ribbons as possible.

Carry your trim to extra lengths on a hooded tee. The highlights on the woven trim at the hem echo the glitter of gold around the hood and neckline.

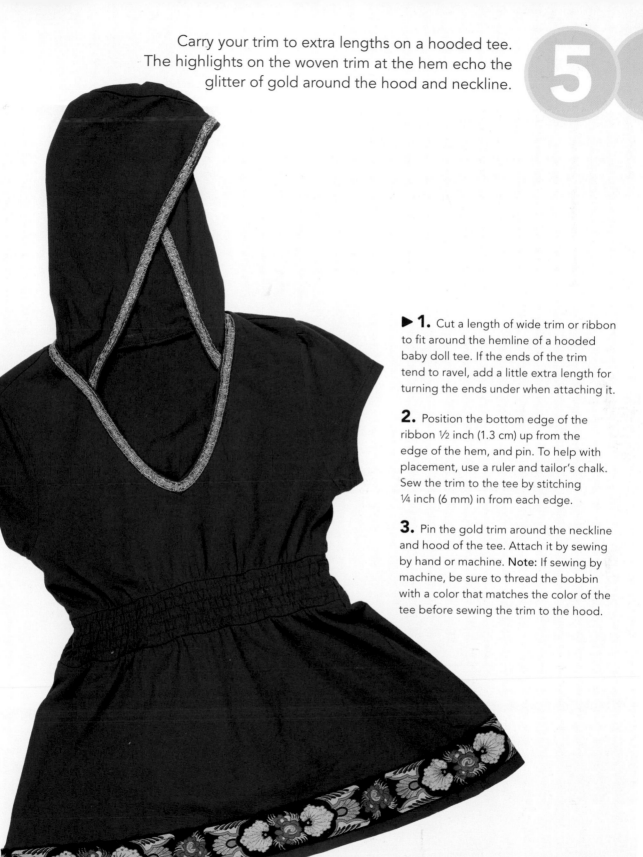

▶ **1.** Cut a length of wide trim or ribbon to fit around the hemline of a hooded baby doll tee. If the ends of the trim tend to ravel, add a little extra length for turning the ends under when attaching it.

2. Position the bottom edge of the ribbon ½ inch (1.3 cm) up from the edge of the hem, and pin. To help with placement, use a ruler and tailor's chalk. Sew the trim to the tee by stitching ¼ inch (6 mm) in from each edge.

3. Pin the gold trim around the neckline and hood of the tee. Attach it by sewing by hand or machine. **Note:** If sewing by machine, be sure to thread the bobbin with a color that matches the color of the tee before sewing the trim to the hood.

Make your own ribbon from bias-cut strips of fabric. I made sheer, silky ribbon to embellish this sweet camisole, but you can experiment with any fabric, from cotton prints to knits.

TATTERED RIBBONS

▶ **1.** Use 1 yard (.9 m) of sheer silk organza or synthetic silk fabric. Cut strips on the bias that are 1 inch (2.5 cm) wide. Use your fingers to fray the raw edges of the strips by pulling away a few strands at a time. Sew the strips together to make one long strip.

2. Use a ballpoint needle and matching thread to sew two rows of ribbon across the neckline, one below the other. Stitch down the center of the ribbon. Sew the ribbons close together; you want the edges to support each other to stand upright.

3. For the third row, use a longer length of ribbon and stitch it to the cami as you did for the first two rows. When you get close to the other side of the bodice, swirl and stitch the end of the ribbon to make a free-form flower shape. Do the same for two more rows of ribbon, overlapping the swirls as you stitch to fill out the flower.

Variation
Tattered Curves

Add soft swoops of tattered, bias-cut ribbon across the bodice of your tee to soften the neckline. Pin from one shoulder seam to the other, and stitch down the center of the ribbon. Trim the edges of the ribbons as needed to align with the shoulder seams.

Soft and billowy like puffy clouds, this tattered-ribbon technique looks more difficult than it is. You actually make an appliqué first by stitching the ribbon to a piece of tulle before attaching it to the tee.

► 1. Use 1 yard (.9 m) of sheer silk organza or synthetic silk fabric. Cut strips on the bias that are 1 inch (2.5 cm) wide. Use your fingers to fray the raw edges of the strips by pulling away a few strands at a time. Sew the strips together to make one long strip.

2. Make a pattern for the appliqué from scrap paper. For this design, I wanted an asymmetrical look that wrapped around the neckline to the back. To make the pattern, place the scrap paper over the shirt, trace the shape of the neckline, and then draw the outline of your appliqué. **Note:** You may need to sketch a few shapes until you get one you like.

3. Cut out the pattern, and then use it to cut out the shape from a piece of tulle.

4. Make your appliqué. Machine or hand stitch the ribbon to the tulle in a large loopy design. Working back and forth across the tulle, continue to stitch until you've covered the entire piece. Continue to work rows of ribbons until you achieve the fullness you desire.

5. Attach the appliqué by hand stitching it to the shirt.

STORM CLOUDS

You can find embroidered or jacquard ribbons and trims in a variety of widths and colors. When adding a sleeve accent to a tank, look for trim that is at least 2 inches (5 cm) wide.

▶ **1.** Cut two lengths of 2-inch (5 cm) trim, each 10 inches (25.4 cm) long.

2. Fold and press under both ends of one length of ribbon on the diagonal, with end and edge aligned and wrong sides together. Repeat for the other length of ribbon.

3. Starting at the front of the shirt, pin the end of one ribbon 4 inches (10.2 cm) down from the shoulder seam. Place the ribbon under the band of the sleeve, using approximately a ½-inch (1.3 cm) seam allowance on the edge of the ribbon. Pin the ribbon along the sleeve front to back, then topstitch along the sleeve band to attach. Repeat for the other sleeve.

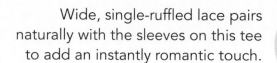

Wide, single-ruffled lace pairs naturally with the sleeves on this tee to add an instantly romantic touch.

BLUSH

▶ **1.** Use single-ruffled lace (page 92) that is 3½ inches (8.9 cm) wide. Measure around the sleeve, and then subtract 5 inches (12.7 cm) from that measurement. Cut two pieces of lace to that length.

2. Fold the straight edge of one of the lengths of lace under ½ inch (1.3 cm), and press. Center the lace on the sleeve at the shoulder seam. Open the fold and lay the crease along the sleeve seam with right sides together. Pin in place.

3. Attach the lace by hand sewing it along the sleeve seam. Flip the lace to cover the sleeve. Stitch the lace flat against the sleeve along the shoulder seam. Repeat steps 2 and 3 with the remaining piece of lace.

> TIP: If your lace sleeves look too puffy, hand tack the lace to the sleeves in a few places.

Get ready to show off your sassy side in this flower-power tube top. If mini is not your style, you can use this technique on any tee.

MOJITO

▶ **1.** Take apart two matching silk flowers in different colors. Keep the petals and discard any plastic. Layer the petals to make three new flowers. You can layer from large petals to small, alternate colors, or make a large flower by just using the large petals.

2. Cover buttons following the manufacturer's instructions in the button kit. Use a silky fabric that contrasts or complements the colors of the flowers.

3. Position the first flower on the tee. Stitch through all layers to sew a button in the center and attach the flower to the tee. Repeat for the remaining flowers.

Variation
Tangerine Sunshine
Make a button flower with one layer of petals and a large button. Look for buttons with bold patterns to accentuate a simple flower.

Time to dig into your overflowing button jar and come up with some magic. Attaching buttons to a tee ensures instant success.

HAPPY BUTTONS

▶ **1.** Have fun positioning a handful of buttons on an area of your tee. Use fabric glue or a fabric glue stick to temporarily attach the buttons to the shirt.

2. Sew the buttons to the tee. **Note:** I matched the thread to the color of the large green button to tie the design together.

> TIP: Try making one button the focal point of your design. For this tee, I used one large, green, vintage button, and then surrounded it with a variety of 28 yellow ones.

● **Variation**
Ahoy Mate

Show off a collection of vintage buttons by sewing a cluster of them together on a tee that complements the theme.

CHAPTER 7

IRON-ONS & PATCHES

All you need is a few minutes—and your iron or sewing machine—to take a tee from drab to delicious. Look for iron-on letters, premade designs, inkjet transfers, and patches at craft and fabric stores. Even vintage clothing can yield some amazing finds.

BASICS

Iron-Ons

Different brands of iron-ons and transfers come with their own set of directions. For best results, always follow the manufacturer's instructions for use and care.

Start with a washed T-shirt. Do not use fabric softener because it may prevent the iron-on or transfer from adhering to the shirt. Iron the tee to remove any wrinkles, but don't use steam. Work on a hard, heat-proof surface when you're fusing the iron-on or transfer, and only press it for the recommended time.

Letters

It used to be that iron-on letters and numbers only came in generic fonts. Today, manufacturers have taken a cue from designer clothing and fashion trends. You can find fonts that glitter or resemble tattoos, and letters can be soft and flocked, or made with embroidered metallics.

Most packages of iron-on letters and numbers contain a few extra. I always recommend you plan your design before you go shopping. That way, you'll know exactly how many packages you'll need to purchase.

Before you fuse the letters or numbers to your tee, take time to arrange them on your shirt to get them exactly where you want them. To make sure they're evenly spaced, begin with the center letter and work from there. Use a clear ruler to measure the distance between each letter or number.

If you want your line of letters to be straight, use a guideline of low-tack masking tape. But be careful when ironing; you never want to iron over the tape. For a whimsical look, make the letters a bit curved or crooked.

Premade Designs

Many manufacturers offer iron-ons that are ready to go. All you'll need is an iron and a pressing cloth. You can find iron-ons that are matte, flocked, glitzy, and even beaded. Look for them in craft or fabric shops, or search the huge inventory you can find online.

Q: *Do you have any tips for laundering tees with patches or iron-ons?*

A: For best results, launder the T-shirt inside out in cold water and hang to dry, or tumble dry on low heat.

Q: *Can I repurpose patches?*

A: If you love a patch that's attached to a tee, tote, or other item that's past its prime, you can easily cut around the patch and reuse it for a new design.

Inkjet Transfers

To create a truly personalized T-shirt, inkjet transfers are the way to go. An inkjet transfer is really just a specialized paper that you use with your inkjet printer. Basically you can transfer whatever you can print off your computer, like family photos or vintage images. Once you've printed the image, you use an iron to transfer it to your fabric. You can find transfer papers at office supply stores, craft stores, and fabric shops.

Regular transfer paper is perfect when working with white or light-colored clothing. However, when you're working with dark fabrics, look for transfer paper made especially for them. One downfall to ink jet transfers is that most retail brands will only stand up to about 20 washings.

Patches

Most patches available in retail stores are iron-ons; all you need is a household iron to attach them. Follow the manufacturer's instructions and you can't go wrong.

Generally, attaching them follows a simple process. First, place the patch glue side down in the desired position on the T-shirt. Then place a pressing cloth over the patch, and iron without steam, using firm pressure. Next, turn the tee inside out and iron the back of the patch. Finally, for extra security, you can use a needle and thread to hand tack the edges of the patch to the T-shirt.

To attach vintage patches and those that aren't self-adhesive, sew around the edges using a coordinating thread. Most patches have a seamed edge that's easy to sew through and makes the stitches virtually undetectable. For larger patches, use fabric glue or a glue stick to hold the patch in place while stitching.

If you want to create your own custom patch, use felt or fleece with inkjet transfers. Keep in mind that not all patches have to be patches. Woven labels and crocheted flowers can also serve the purpose.

Send a message using a package or two of iron-on letters. Be sure to plan ahead by checking the letter count in the package to make sure you have enough.

LET IT SNOW

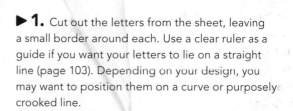

▶ **1.** Cut out the letters from the sheet, leaving a small border around each. Use a clear ruler as a guide if you want your letters to lie on a straight line (page 103). Depending on your design, you may want to position them on a curve or purposely crooked line.

2. Follow the manufacturer's instructions for attaching the letters to the tee.

Variation
The Great 1988

Oversized, distressed numbers make a bold statement when attached to the back of a T-shirt. This design was fashioned after my graduation year. Other ideas for putting numbers on tees are birthday celebrations, sports numbers, wedding dates, family reunions, and anniversaries.

Matte iron-ons have a flat, smooth texture. They generally have lots of color and detail, which makes them fun to use.

TAKING FLIGHT

▶ 1. Begin with either individual iron-ons or a full-sheet design. If you want to use just a portion of a full-sheet design, cut out the motifs you want to use, leaving a small border around them.

2. Position the iron-on where you want it. Follow the manufacturer's instructions for attaching it to the tee.

> TIP: Be careful when washing shirts with matte iron-ons, since the iron-ons tend to crack with heat. You'll get better results by hand washing the shirt in cold water, and then hanging it to dry.

● Variation
Blue Bird Silhouette

Flocked iron-ons are soft and fuzzy and meant to be touched. Their velvety texture is rich and luxurious on a plain tee. For this shirt, I used seven identical iron-ons to create this large design. If needed, cut the motifs from a full sheet, leaving a small border around each. Place the iron-ons in the desired position on the front of the T-shirt, and then follow the manufacturer's instructions for attaching them to the fabric.

Faux or no? You can find iron-ons that look exactly like fabric appliqués. Use them when you want a no-sew alternative to decorating your tee.

▶ **1.** Place the iron-on at the desired position on the front of your T-shirt.

2. Follow the manufacturer's instructions for attaching it to the fabric, and you're done!

This iron-on has the look of detailed beadwork without the fuss. In fact, it looked so much like a real brooch I placed it on the collar of the tee.

CHERRY BOMB

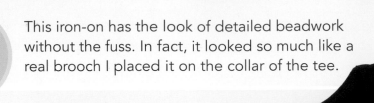

▶ **1.** Place the iron-on in the desired position on the T-shirt. Follow the manufacturer's instructions for attaching it to the fabric.

2. Take care when laundering tees with beaded iron-ons. Be sure to hand wash them, and hang them to dry.

Find a digital image, create one with design software, or scan an image into your computer. Print it on inkjet transfer paper, and you're ready to decorate your tee.

►1. Use photo-editing software to resize or crop clip art of a person knitting or use the pattern on page 171. If the image has words, make sure you flip the image to get a mirror image so the words come out correctly when transferred to the tee.

2. Print the design on inkjet transfer paper, and cut it out. Follow the manufacturer's instructions for transferring it to the fabric.

> TIP: Save money on transfer paper when working with small motifs for different designs. Try printing several small images on one sheet, and then cut them out when needed.

IRON-ONS & PATCHES

Make sure you use inkjet transfer paper made especially for use on dark fabrics when working on a dark tee. Most of the time, you won't need to flip images with words as you do for transfers for light fabric.

▶ **1.** Use photo-editing software to resize or crop clip art of a vintage Paris postcard.

2. Print the design on inkjet transfer paper made for use on dark fabric, and then cut it out. Use scalloped or pinking shears to cut a decorative edge around the transfer. Follow the manufacturer's instructions for transferring it to the fabric.

3. Sew on a small fleur-de-lis patch for extra embellishment.

> TIP: Keep your transferred tee looking good by hand washing it and hanging it to dry.

PARIS IS JUST A FLIGHT AWAY

Use inkjet transfers over printed fabrics to add dimension to your tee. Shirts printed in light colors pair best with bold inkjet designs in contrasting colors.

▶ **1.** Use photo-editing software to design an image in contrasting colors to those on your selected tee. If the image has words, make sure you flip the image to get a mirror image so the words come out correctly when transferred to the tee.

2. Print the design on inkjet transfer paper, and cut it out. Follow the manufacturer's instructions for transferring it to the fabric.

Sleeves are the perfect place to showcase a collection of patches. Overlap them, line them up straight, or wrap them around a cuff.

STAR SHINE

▶ **1.** Working with three star patches, position them up the sleeve of a tee. Overlap the patches a little for added interest.

2. If you're using iron-on patches, follow the manufacturer's instructions for attaching them to the tee. If not, attach them with fabric glue or by hand stitching them to the fabric.

● **Variation**

Love

If you have short hair, or wear your hair in a ponytail, place your patch toward the top center back. You're sure to get lots of compliments.

This little owl needed a perch. By adding paint, embroidery, ribbon, or even rhinestones to your design, you can give a patch the extra detail it needs to succeed.

▶ **1.** On the front of your tee, use strips of masking tape to tape off a design that resembles an organic-looking tree branch. Use brown fabric paint to fill in the exposed area. Allow to dry. Follow the manufacturer's instructions for heat setting the paint.

2. If the patch is an iron-on, follow the manufacturer's instructions for attaching it to the tee. If not, attach it with fabric glue or by hand stitching it to the fabric.

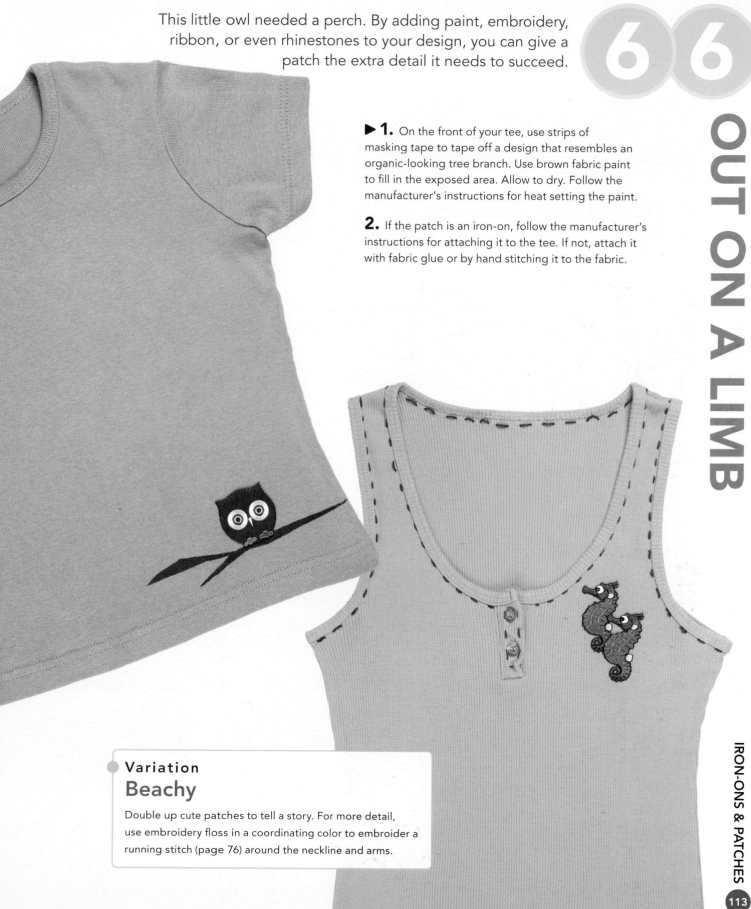

● **Variation**
Beachy

Double up cute patches to tell a story. For more detail, use embroidery floss in a coordinating color to embroider a running stitch (page 76) around the neckline and arms.

CHAPTER 8

SPARKLE & SHINE

Take an everyday tee, add a bit of bling, and then go out and strut your stuff. It doesn't matter if you hit the clubs or the grocery store. Share the glamour wherever you go.

BASICS

Bring on the Bling

I admit it. I'm a sparkle junkie! I love all things that glitter, shimmer, and shine. I'm one of those gals who believes there's no such thing as too many rhinestones or sequins. When I discovered how to bring the bling to plain or printed tees, I knew I'd found my calling.

Loose Rhinestones

Loose rhinestones add color and shimmer to any design. Purchase them at local craft and fabric stores or online. I've found online retailers carry the widest selection.

Look for stones made of crystal or acrylic with flat backs. Crystal stones have a brilliant shine and are the most expensive. Acrylic stones are less expensive and slightly less shiny than crystal stones. Both work equally well for embellishing a tee.

You can find stones in every color and in different finishes. Rhinestones marked AB (aurora borealis) have a rainbow effect, and those marked SC have special coatings or cuts.

Stones come in different sizes measured in millimeters; the smallest being 1.8 mm and the largest 35 mm, roughly the size of a quarter. You can find rounds, squares, teardrops, hearts, emerald cuts, and even specialty shapes.

You attach rhinestones using a gem-setting tool or machine, a hot-wand applicator, or gem glue. Setting tools and machines have been around for years and work by piercing the fabric. If you're adding lots of stones, this may not be the best choice for knit fabrics. I prefer using hot wands on tees. They work by heating the glue on glue-treated stones that you attach directly to the fabric. The wand comes with a set of interchangeable tips to accommodate different sizes of stones.

When using gem glue, look for products that are nontoxic, washable, and designed for adhering porous and semi-porous surfaces together. A little glue goes a long way, so don't buy the giant economy size.

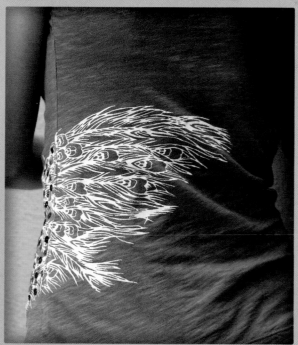

Metal Studs

Sophisticates as well as rock-and-roll gladiators appreciate the design appeal of metal studs. They're perfect for adding a little glitz without the sparkle. Studs are available in different shapes, sizes, and metal finishes. They have prongs on the back that pierce and then grip the fabric when bent. You can purchase studs in kits that include a tool for attaching them. You can also attach them using a gem-setting tool or machine, a hot-wand applicator, or gem glue.

Iron-ons

Sparkly iron-ons allow you to glam-up your tee in no time. Look for a variety of bejeweled designs including those with words, hearts, skulls, team logos, animals, tattoos, and flowers. When you attach rhinestone and studded iron-ons, carefully follow the manufacturer's instructions. If you use too much or too little heat, your stones will not adhere properly.

Rhinestone Trim

You can find trim embellished with rhinestones at specialty costume and fabric stores. You attach it with fabric glue or by hand sewing it to the fabric. This trim can be costly, so plan ahead by measuring out exactly how much you need before you go shopping.

Q & A

Q: What's the best way to store loose rhinestones?

A: I keep my stones, sorted by color and size, in clear-plastic divider boxes. You can also keep tiny rhinestones in small zip-top plastic bags.

Q: How can I prevent glue from seeping around the edges of the stones?

A: Place a small amount of glue on a piece of wax paper, dip the head of a pin into it, and then dot the glue onto the tee at the desired position. Using the pin prevents you from using too much glue. Attach your rhinestone, and allow the glue to dry.

Paints

Metallic, pearl, and glitter fabric paint add excitement to your designs. When working with paints, be sure to tuck a piece of wax paper inside the tee. This simple step prevents the paint from seeping to the other side. Since fabric paints need to be heat set prior to laundering, follow the manufacturer's instructions. Look for their care guidelines as well.

Sequins

You can find sequins at any craft and fabric store. They're so reasonably priced that every embellisher should have jars full. Glue them on with gem glue or stitch them by hand. You can also purchase sewn sequins by the yard.

Rhinestone Buttons

Buy these in either sew-through or shank styles. They make a perfect statement when centered on a silk-flower embellishment.

Highlight the neckline of a tee by attaching studs using a hand-held setting tool. You can also attach studs with glue or a heat wand.

▶ **1.** Working on the right side of the tee, place the stud in the desired position. Pierce the fabric with the prongs. Continue holding the stud in place as you turn the fabric to the wrong side.

2. Position the hand-held setter over the prongs and press until the prongs bend, attaching the stud to the fabric.

68

Use a heat wand to attach a spray of tiny glue-treated rhinestones to your tee. I used two different shades of purple stones in two different sizes; the smaller ones complement the delicate pattern of the tee.

CHERRY BLOSSOMS

▶ **1.** Attach a tip on the heat wand that corresponds to the size stone you're using. Place the stone in the tip with its glue side facing out. Following the manufacturer's instructions, work on a heatproof surface to attach the stone to the tee.

2. After you've finished attaching the stones of one size, allow the wand to cool, and then replace the tip. Repeat step 1 until you've attached all remaining stones.

Variation
Morning Sun

Gluing rhinestones to a printed tee is one of the easiest ways to bring the bling. Slide a piece of wax paper inside the tee to prevent glue from seeping through to the other side. Place a small amount of gem glue on a piece of wax paper, dip the head of a straight pin into the glue, and dot the glue onto the tee. Attach the rhinestones, and allow the glue to dry.

Variation
Seafood

Use a gem-setting tool to attach rhinestones. Each tool is a bit different, so be sure to follow the manufacturer's instructions for use. Generally, you first position a separate pronged back into the arm of the machine before placing the rhinestone, bottom up, in the rounded well. You lay the tee wrong side up over the stone, and then press the arm down to bend the prongs that attach it to the fabric.

Look for rhinestone iron-ons that feature specific shapes or those that spell out fun and flirty words. Choose from the large variety found at craft and fabric shops.

TATTOO LOVE

▶ **1.** Remove the backing sheet from the iron-on. Place it on the desired location on the T-shirt. Follow the manufacturer's instructions for attaching it to the fabric.

2. Be careful when ironing. Too much or too little heat and the stones will not adhere properly.

● **Variation**
Fearless Girl

Got a sporty girl who also loves a touch of glamour? Make a tee that honors the best of both her worlds. This design looks great on a sport tee.

Some tees are meant for teasing! This little cutie is embellished to the nines with rhinestone trim, embroidered flowers, and a silhouette patch.

▶ **1.** Working on a lace-trimmed camisole, hand stitch a strip of rhinestone trim following the front neckline. Be sure to use a thread color that matches the lace trim.

2. Decorate the side hemline with a silhouette or other girly iron-on patch (page 103).

3. Hand stitch a small flower detail at the center front of the cami's neckline. Sew another one on the silhouette patch.

● Variation
Whisper

A little goes a long way! Add a permanent brooch to a simple tee by hand sewing or gluing a short, wide strip of rhinestones to a deep V-neck or scoop-neck tee.

Two shades of paint, highlighted in gold and finished with an iridescent coat, make these butterflies come to life. The dimensional gold glitter paint adds texture and depth.

▶ **1.** Slide a piece of wax paper inside the tee to prevent paint from seeping through to the other side.

2. Using a round paintbrush, paint the butterflies with the purple and plum metallic fabric paint. Tap any excess paint from the brush, and use a light hand when painting. Don't worry about filling in the whole butterfly. Allow the paint to dry.

3. Pour dimensional gold glitter fabric paint onto a piece of wax paper. Use the round brush to highlight the inner edges of the wings. Allow to dry.

4. Pour iridescent paint onto a piece of wax paper. Using the round brush, paint the entire wing. Allow to dry.

5. Follow the manufacturer's instructions for heat setting the paint.

> TIP: Paint some of the butterflies with only gold and iridescent paints to add more visual interest to the overall design.

Variation
Peace and Love

Try silkscreening (page 29) with metallic paints to add sparkle to your design. Layer prints and colors to create an allover pattern, or use just one screen for a simple, graphic look.

PEACE

Gluing is the fastest way to attach sequins when covering a large area. For small or delicate areas, sew the sequins to the tee by hand.

▶ **1.** Slide a piece of wax paper inside the tee to prevent glue from seeping through to the other side.

2. Place a small amount of gem glue on a piece of wax paper, dip the head of a straight pin into the glue, and dot the glue over the silkscreen design on the tee. Place the sequins on the glue where desired, and allow to dry.

● **Variation**
Sailor Girl

Hand sewing sequins is much easier than it looks. Double thread a needle, and knot the end. Working on the inside of the tee, bring the thread to the front, leaving the knot on the inside. Place a sequin on the needle. Next add a seed bead. Bring the needle back through the hole. Continue adding sequins and beads until you are happy with the design. Knot the end of the thread when you're finished. For the sleeves, slit the top of each sleeve from hem to shoulder seam. Pass a length of ribbon under each shoulder seam, and then tie a bow on each.

Sequined appliqués always remind me of elaborate ice-dancing or circus costumes. Let their playful spirit brighten your tee.

ICE

▶ **1.** Remove one shoulder of a tank top. Lay the tank on a flat work surface. Begin at one underarm seam and cut through both layers across the tee at an angle to the other strap.

2. Fold the raw edges under, and hem by using matching thread to topstitch.

3. Overlap individual, sequined, leaf-shape appliqués on the remaining strap. Use fabric glue to hold them in place. After the glue dries, sew around the appliqués by hand, if needed, to secure them.

● **Variation**
Night Blooming

Add a waist detail to a baby doll or gathered tee. Position a sequined appliqué on the desired position at the waistline. Attach it with fabric glue or sew it to the tee by hand using matching thread. If the appliqué is an iron-on, follow the manufacturer's instructions for attaching it to the tee.

If you believe you can never have enough sequins, buy it by the yard. You can find sequined fabric, trims embellished with sequins, and strands of single sequins in every color.

LIMEADE

▶ **1.** Buy floral lace trim already embellished with sequins, and a strand of sequins to serve as a highlight.

2. Attach the lace trim along the front hem and at the center of the neckline to swoop up and just over the shoulder. Complete the design by randomly snaking the strand of sequins back and forth across the neckline.

SPARKLE & SHINE

125

CHAPTER 9

MIXED MEDIA

Combine different techniques and materials to make your own mixed-media mash-ups. You don't have to play by the rules when creating these looks. All you need are a few tips for success before you begin.

BASICS

Plan Ahead

You've learned lots of different techniques for altering a tee. Now it's time to combine them to create even more exciting looks. The best advice for the success of your design is to plan ahead by thinking in layers; begin with the first layer, then build out to completion.

First Things First

When designing a mixed-media tee, list the techniques you'll use. Then ask yourself some questions. For example, if you decide to work with paints, iron-ons, and embroidery, decide which element of the design is the first layer, the task you need to complete first to build your design. Will the painted portion be under the iron-on, surround it, or will you paint directly on it? Will you embroider only the T-shirt fabric or also the iron-on? Once you've figured it out, begin with the first design layer and work your way to the finishing touches. Keep a list if needed, or just lay out your supplies in the order in which you'll work with them.

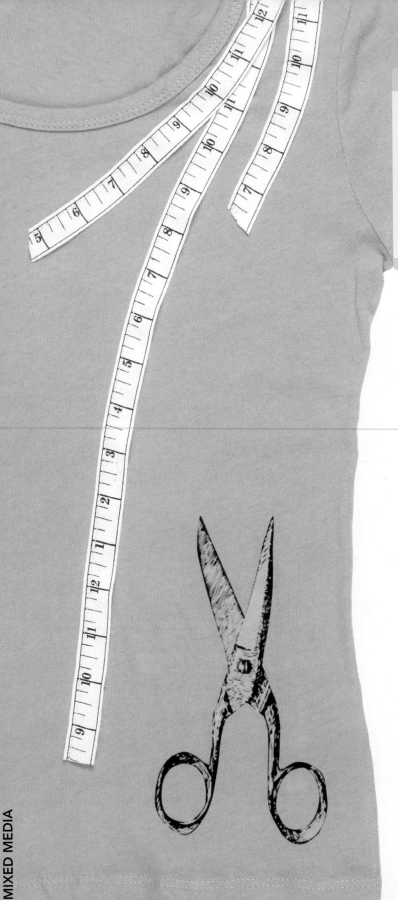

Q: *How do I make all the different media work in one design?*

A: Think about unifying the elements. There are several different ways. You can try working with one color scheme for all the different mediums. Or, decide on one theme to carry through for all elements. Another way is to overlap the mediums, such as embroidery and paint on patches and appliqués.

Be Flexible

I know I just told you to plan ahead, which is still the best way to get started. But don't be surprised if the creative process leads you astray as you work. Don't be afraid of changing your plan. New ideas can lead to better designs. Also, don't be afraid to try something new because you fear failure. Remember, there is no failure, just fun!

Caring for Your Tee

When you're making your design, follow the different instructions from the product manufacturers for each element. Remember to heat set paint as instructed, or follow the time limit for pressing an iron-on to adhere it to the fabric. Because the materials on a mixed-media tee may have different laundering instructions, hand washing and line drying the tee may be the best bet.

Attach a lacy collar appliqué to your tee, then cut away the original neckline for a whole new look. Add a few gathered roses, and you're ready to go.

▶ **1.** Sew a V-neck, lace-collar appliqué by hand to the front of a crew-neck tee. Fold one end of the appliqué under and stitch it to the tee along the shoulder seam. Sew the collar to the tee along the inside edge.

2. When you get to the other shoulder, turn the other end of the collar under and stitch it along the shoulder seam. Then sew the collar to the tee along the outside edge.

3. Cut the crew neck from the T-shirt by cutting as close to the appliqué as possible.

4. Cut three strips from the fabric you removed from the neckline. Make three small gathered roses (page 12) from the strips. Position the roses on the shoulder of the tee, and attach them by sewing a button in the center of each through all layers of fabric.

Bring focus to features or design elements by embroidering a pop of color. For this design, I opted for bright orange eyes.

I ONLY HAVE EYES 4 U

▶ **1.** Copy the skull template on page 171, and cut it out. Use it to cut an appliqué from print fabric. Cut away the heart-shaped eyes. Gently fray the edges for a distressed look.

2. Use the template as a guide to cut another skull shape from a solid fabric. Extend the edges approximately ½ inch (1.3 cm) all around. When you get to the lower-right cross bone, extend the shape of the appliqué into a free-flowing heart shape.

3. Sew the skull to the larger shape. Following the manufacturer's instructions, attach iron-on nailhead studs (page 116) to the extended heart shape.

4. Position the appliqué on the shirt, pin, and then sew to attach.

5. With six strands of orange embroidery floss, use the split stitch (page 76) to embroider an outlined heart in each eye.

Stencils, appliqués, and beads bring a bit of whimsy to this sunny tee. The touch of tulle on the wings creates a subtle 3-D effect.

▶ **1.** Use purchased butterfly stencils and three different colors of fabric paint to stencil a random pattern on one side of the front of a tee (page 28). Follow the manufacturer's instructions for heat setting the paint.

2. Copy the butterfly pattern on page 172, and cut it out. Follow the manufacturer's instructions for fusing paper-backed fusible webbing to scraps of black knit fabric. Use the pattern to cut two butterflies from the fused fabric.

3. Remove the paper backing, and place the appliqués on the tee in the desired positions. Follow the manufacturer's instructions for fusing the appliqués to the tee. Sew around the edges of the appliqués, if desired.

4. Cut two 3-inch (7.6 cm) squares from tulle fabric. Fold each square in half, and gather them at the center before sewing them by hand on the appliquéd butterflies.

5. Sew the beaded antennas. Begin by bringing a threaded beading needle through the fabric from wrong side to right side. Slip 10 to 15 seed beads on the needle. Bring the needle back through the tee approximately 1 inch (2.5 cm) from where you began. Stitch back over the line of beads to secure them to the tee.

An inkjet transfer paired with themed ribbon creates a design that shows off your crafter pride.

CRAFTY

▶ **1.** Copy the template on page 172, scan it into your computer so you can enlarge it, and print it on inkjet transfer paper (page 104). Cut the image out, and then follow the manufacturer's instructions for transferring it to the tee.

2. Pin three lengths of measuring-tape themed ribbon across the shoulder area and extending down the front. Only sew along the left edge of the ribbons to attach them to create a looser ruffled effect.

> TIP: You can save a step if you find a clip art image you like online. That way, it's already in your computer ready to enlarge and print.

Talk about battle of the bands! Start with two rock-and-roll tees. Cut a motif from one for the reverse appliqué on the other, add some iron-on studs and rhinestones, and you're ready to rock.

▶ **1.** You'll need two rock and roll tees. Cut a motif from one of them, and use it to create the reverse appliqué on the other (see Chardonnay on page 73).

2. Follow the manufacturer's instructions for adhering iron-on studs to the tee on the area you wish to highlight.

3. Use gem glue to attach a grouping of rhinestones over any words or motifs for added bling.

80

Wear this T-shirt and sweatshirt combination when sporting around town, grabbing a cup of coffee, or cozying up with a book.

1. You'll need a front-pocket sweatshirt with a ribbed waistband and a three-quarter sleeve or long-sleeve tee. Carefully cut off the ribbed waistband and front pocket from the sweatshirt.

2. Pin the pocket to the front of the tee. Sew entirely around the pocket to attach it to the shirt.

3. Fold the ribbed waistband in half, and cut to make two pieces. Pin one end of one piece at a shoulder seam on the tee. Free-form pleat the strip along the neckline (page 13), pinning as you go, and ending at the center front of the tee.

4. Attach the pleated piece by machine or by hand stitching it, first to the shoulder seam and then along the neckline. Repeat the pleating, pinning, and sewing on the other side of the neckline using the remaining piece of waistband.

5. Cut a length of seam binding that is twice the length of the front of the neckline measured from shoulder to shoulder. Pin one end of the seam binding on top of the pleated ribbing at a shoulder seam.

6. Free-form pleat the binding along the entire length of the neckline, pinning as you go. Attach the pleated binding by machine or by hand stitching it to the shoulder seam and along the neckline.

7. Attach a length of decorative trim or braiding over the stitching line on the pleated seam binding. You can attach it with fabric glue or sew it as preferred.

Variation
Dainty

Soft and sweet, this little number will turn heads. Start with a tank that has crocheted trim on the straps and neckline. Thread a long piece of seam binding or ribbon through the openings in the crocheted pattern. Once you've circled the neckline and straps, tie the ends. Use gem glue to attach a grouping of colored rhinestones to the center of a silk flower petal. Allow the glue to dry, and then sew the flower on top of the ends.

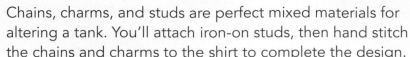

81

Chains, charms, and studs are perfect mixed materials for altering a tank. You'll attach iron-on studs, then hand stitch the chains and charms to the shirt to complete the design.

CAMEO

▶ **1.** Follow the manufacturer's instructions for attaching gold iron-on studs to one strap and a bit of the yoke on a tank top (page 116).

2. Sew one end of a length of chunky chain to one shoulder seam on the tank. Drape the chain in a graceful scoop along the neckline of the tank. Sew the other end of the chain to the other shoulder seam. **Note:** You may need to remove links from your length of chain to get the look you desire.

3. Secure the chain to the tank by hand stitching it in a few places along the straps. Attach a second, shorter length of chain to the first.

4. Decide where you want to place your charms along the strap with the studs. Attach the charms by hand sewing them to the tank. Take the stitches through a link on the chain and the fabric when sewing each one to the shirt.

5. Care for the tee by washing it by hand and hanging it to dry.

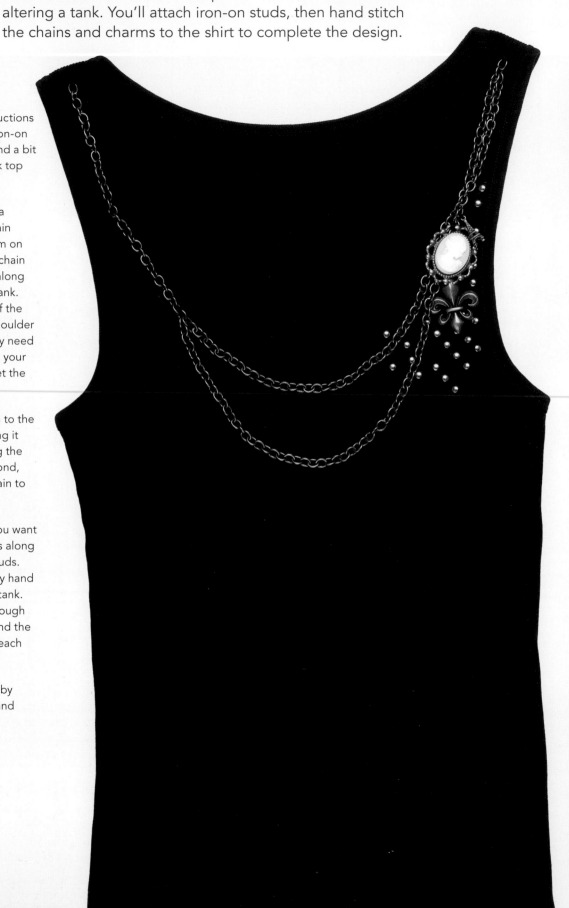

No wipe out here. Shabby-surf is chic! Cut a motif from one shirt to appliqué on the other. Then add embroidery and a ribboned iron-on patch to complete the look.

▶ **1.** You'll need one shabby tee and one distressed surfer tee. Cut a motif from the surfer tee. Use a sewing machine to appliqué it on the shabby tee.

2. Embroider freehand over the appliqué and down the sides of the tee. Use a combination of stitches—whipstitch, straight stitch, and backstitch (pages 76 to 77).

3. Machine embroider for extra texture by using the zigzag stitch in a free-form manner—just allow the stitches to go where they take you. Use a matching thread or go wild with bright color.

4. Follow the manufacturer's instructions for attaching a ribbon-embellished iron-on patch to the tee.

83

Peace out! Reinvent an icon of the 1960s for today's hippie girl. Tie-dye, patches, and a sequined iron-on unite to make this peace-loving design.

► **1.** Tie-dye a T-shirt with targets using hot-pink dye (see Rainbow Rays on page 56).

2. Follow the manufacturer's instructions for attaching a large, sequined, iron-on peace sign to the lower corner of the tee. Use a pressing cloth to prevent scorching the sequins.

3. Sew, glue, or iron on layers of hippie-inspired patches to the tee.

Let the print on the scarf determine the stamp and stencil for the painted design. For this project, it's all about the stars.

STAR LIGHT

▶ **1.** Cut 1-inch (2.5 cm) vertical slits, evenly spacing them apart, along the neckline of either a V-neck or crew-neck T-shirt. Thread a scarf through the slits, and tie it in a knot or bow at the center front of the shirt.

2. Using a star-shaped foam stamp, print a star in the lower front corner of the tee (page 29). Allow the paint to dry.

3. Use a stencil with multiple small stars to stencil a design over the larger star (page 28), and allow to dry. Follow the manufacturer's instructions for heat setting the paint.

CHAPTER 10

JUST THE BOYS

Have you ever been stumped when it came to crafting a gift for a guy? If so, you've come to the right place. In this chapter, you can mix media to make tees that any boy or guy will love.

BASICS

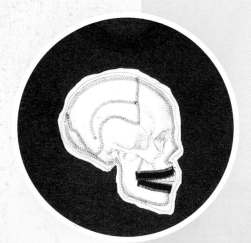

Fitting the Profile

Guys love getting handmade gifts, especially when they are as cool looking as these tees. The trick is figuring out the perfect match between T-shirt and fella. Use the following guide to make your job easier. Whether you're crafting for your pop, boyfriend, hubby, son, or best friend, you're sure to find a design that fits his personality.

Trekkie Techie

If your guy is all-things-technical or a sci-fi fan, try making SR-71 (page 150) or They Came from Space (page 143). One uses the reverse appliqué technique, the other uses bleach and shelf liner to make the design—which kind of sounds like its own science experiment.

Sports Zombie

You know the type. He eats, breathes, and talks sports around the clock. For racing fans, try making Racer Mike (page 145), which uses embroidered name patches for a personalized touch. It'll make him feel like a member of the pit crew. If football reigns supreme in your guy's real or fantasy realm, Football Star (page 149) is a mixed-media design made with embroidery and paint.

Working-Class Hero

Even working guys will love a personalized tee. It's your way of saying you appreciate all he does. Look for Hammer Time (page 153) and Off to Work (page 148). Your man might not know an appliqué from a patch, but hey, who cares.

I'm a Blues Man

If music makes your man go round, then Bootleg Tapes (page 151) is sure to please. Bright green tie-dye and a funky patch is all you need to complete this design. If you're lucky enough to have concert patches or band logos, you can further customize the design. Don't forget that little boys like music, too. My Dad Rocks (page 144), Mini Rocker (page 147), and Born to Rock (page 152) say it all.

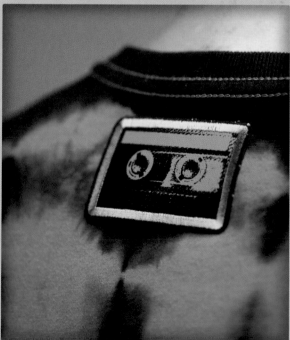

Art Aficionado

Artsy guys appreciate mixed media—the more complex, the better. You can layer on the meaning when you make Chatter Box (page 146). It uses inkjet transfers, dimensional stitching, and 3-D zipper teeth. You have to see it to believe it.

Mr. Question Mark

If your guy doesn't fit any of the above profiles, use the designs as a springboard for your own creations. Mix and match ideas or strike out on your own. No matter how you stitch it, paint it, or embellish it, any man in your life, young or old, is going to love a handmade tee crafted by you.

Q & A

Q: *Will I be able to find enough guy-themed products for altering tees?*

A: Not a problem. Gals might make up most of the crafting population, but even manufacturers know guys hold up half the sky.

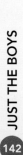

Use bleach to undye a black tee. The robot stencil made from self-adhesive shelf liner will make any techie proud.

85

THEY CAME FROM SPACE

▶ **1.** Copy the template on page 173, and cut it out. Use it as a guide to trace a stencil on self-adhesive shelf liner (page 28). Cut out the rays and robot.

2. Lay the tee flat on a protected work surface. Place a piece of wax paper inside the tee between the front and back to prevent the bleach from seeping through.

3. Peel the backing from the cutout rays and robot, and stick them to the tee using the photo as a guide for placement. Press the edges with your fingers.

4. Add a small amount of bleach to a spray bottle used only for bleach. Spray the bleach over the stencil; work quickly. Allow the tee to sit until you begin to see the color change. Note: Remember to protect your clothing from the bleach.

5. As soon as the color begins to change, rinse the tee with cold water and a little detergent to deactivate the bleach. Rinse the shirt again, and hang or tumble dry.

Mine your old T-shirts for appliqué ideas. Look for shirts with motifs that inspire you, or slice up dad's tees to create new looks for little boys.

▶ **1.** Cut out a motif from an old, clean T-shirt. Leave at least a 1-inch (2.5 cm) allowance around the edges.

2. Cut lightweight, paper-backed fusible webbing to fit the motif. Follow the manufacturer's instructions to fuse the webbing to the wrong side of the fabrics.

3. Cut out the motifs by cutting away most of the allowance you left in step 1. Remove the paper backing and place the appliqués on the tee in the desired positions. Follow the manufacturer's instructions to fuse the appliqués to the tee. If needed, use a pressing cloth over the motifs.

4. Thread your machine with regular or satin thread, and use a straight, zigzag, or satin stitch to sew around the edges (page 60).

Girls call them ribbons; guys call them racing stripes. Create a sporty tee by adding tri-color ribbon and a personalized name patch.

RACER MIKE

▶ **1.** Cut a length of ribbon to fit down the side of a tee. Add a little extra to each end for folding them under to prevent raveling.

2. Use a water-soluble fabric marker to draw a vertical line on the front of the shirt approximately 4 inches (10.2 cm) in from the side seam. Fold the ends of the ribbon under. Use a fabric glue stick to position the ribbon over the marked line.

3. Attach the ribbon to the shirt by sewing it along each long edge. Use a coordinating colored thread to make the stitches invisible.

4. Center the name patch on the ribbon approximately 2 to 3 inches (5 to 7.6 cm) up from the bottom of the hem. Iron-on or sew the patch to the tee.

If you want to impress a cool, artsy guy, make him an edgy T-shirt. Add to the layers of meaning by giving the inkjet transfer a 3-D effect with wild stitching and zipper teeth.

CHATTER BOX

▶ **1.** Copy the template of the skull on page 172, and scan it into your computer. Use photo-editing software to resize or crop the image.

2. Print the design on inkjet transfer paper, and cut it out. Follow the manufacturer's instructions for transferring the image to a light-colored knit fabric. Cut the image out, leaving a small border around the edge.

3. Position the skull in the center of the tee. Use your sewing machine with navy thread to stitch around the skull to attach it to the tee. Add decorative zigzag stitches on the skull using navy and turquoise thread.

4. Cut a length as long as the teeth on the skull from a black metal zipper. Place one of the strips along the lower jaw and one above. Use a zigzag stitch on your sewing machine to sew through the zipper tape to attach the strips to the skull.

> **TIP:** Save yourself a step by finding a skull image online since it will already be in your computer. If you use an image with words, be sure to flip it to get a mirror image so the words will read correctly when transferred to the fabric.

A silkscreen, a little paint, and you're ready to rock! Even little boys know how good they look wearing a cool T-shirt.

89

▶ **1.** Position a rocker-themed silkscreen on the tee. Note: Try out premade designs available at craft shops, or design your own (page 29).

2. Place a dollop of lime green silkscreen paint at the center of the guitar. Run a bead of black silkscreen paint across the top of the screen. Use the squeegee

to pull the paint down the screen. Lift the screen. Allow the paint to dry before heat setting it following the manufacturer's instructions.

3. Use the backstitch (page 76) to embroider the guitar strings with bright orange embroidery floss.

MINI ROCKER

Whether your guy prefers tees or ties, he'll love this shirt. Customize the tee by choosing a cotton print for the appliqué that mirrors his special interest or hobby.

OFF TO WORK

▶ **1.** Copy the tie templates on page 173, and cut them out. Follow the manufacturer's instructions for fusing lightweight, paper-backed fusible webbing to your fabric.

2. Use the templates as a pattern to cut the shapes from the fused fabric.

3. Remove the paper backing, and place the appliqués on the tee in the desired position. Follow the manufacturer's instructions for fusing the appliqué to the tee.

4. Thread your machine with regular or satin thread, and use the straight, zigzag, or satin stitch to sew around the edges of the appliqué.

● **Variation**
I'm Five!

Kids of all ages will love having a custom B-day tee to wear on their special day. Make a birthday tee by appliquéing the date or age on the front of the shirt. Use stencils or templates made from letters and numbers printed from computer fonts.

Combine stenciling and embroidery to make a special shirt for game day. You can find images from any sport to inspire your design. To show you really care, make the tee using his team colors.

▶ **1.** Use embroidery transfer paper to copy the template on page 173. Transfer the motif to the tee at the desired location. Embroider the outline of the motif using machine or hand embroidery.

2. Use stencils and black fabric paint to paint the words on the shirt. Before removing the stencils, brush over the edges of the stencils for a distressed look. Allow the paint to dry, and then follow the manufacturer's instructions for heat setting the paint.

3. Highlight the letters by embroidering over them using the backstitch (page 76) with six strands of embroidery floss. **Note:** Light colors of floss work best over black.

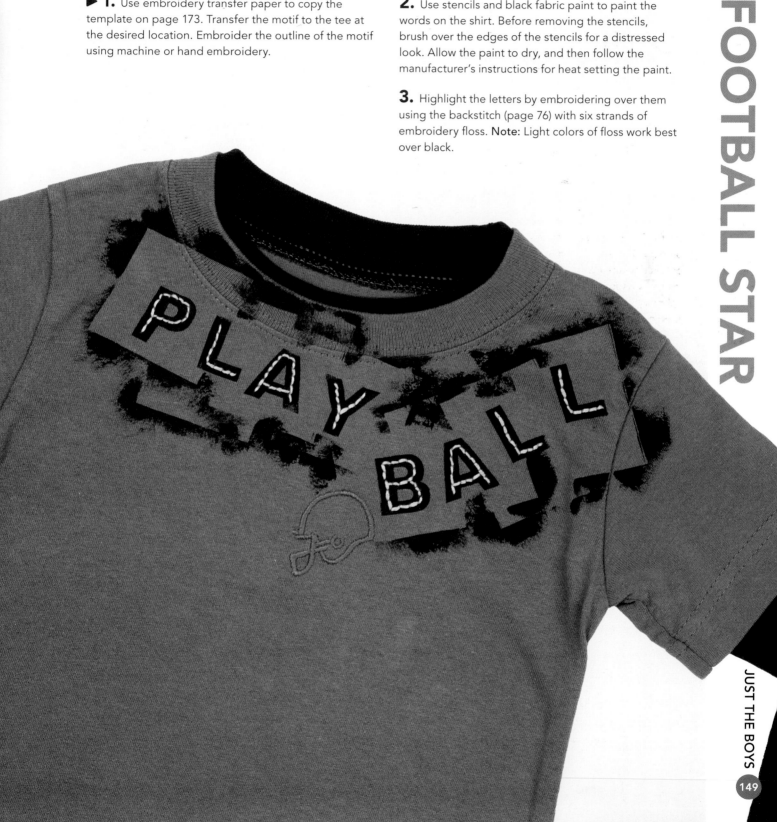

For reverse appliqué, you cut away a portion of the shirt to reveal the appliqué underneath. It's a great way to repurpose his favorite stained shirt.

SR-71

▶ **1.** Cut out a motif from a cotton print or old T-shirt. Leave at least a 1-inch (2.5 cm) allowance around the edges.

2. Turn the T-shirt inside out, and lay it front side up. Pin the motif right side down to the wrong side of the tee in the desired position.

3. Sew through both layers following the edge of the appliqué.

4. Turn the tee right side out. Approximately ½ inch (1.3 cm) in from the stitching line, cut away the knit fabric to reveal the appliqué underneath.

5. Add extra detail by sewing a second cutout to the tee or by adding a few patches.

What would a summer concert be without a few tie-dyed tees in the audience? Add some patches to the design, buy the tickets, and rock on.

BOOTLEG TAPES

▶ **1.** Dye the stripes (see Camp Navy on page 53). Wet a prewashed, green T-shirt. Lay the tee on a flat work surface. Starting at the hem, gather accordion pleats up the entire shirt, including the sleeves.

2. Pinch a section of the shirt together at the center and tightly wrap it with a rubber band or two. Create a second stripe by wrapping a few more rubber bands next to the first one. Continue until stripes of rubber bands encircle the shirt from one side to the other.

3. Following the dye bath instructions on page 46, prepare a dark green dye bath.

4. Dip the tee into the prepared dye bath, and soak it until it reaches the desired color. Remove it from the bath, rinse it, and then use scissors to cut away the rubber bands.

5. Rinse the tee, roll it in an old towel to remove the excess water, and hang to dry.

6. Follow the manufacturer's instructions to attach a music-themed iron-on patch to the center of the upper back.

Even babies can get in on the trend for designer tees. With the simple addition of an iron-on, you can embellish adult T-shirts, kids' tees, and snapsuits for babies in five minutes or less.

BORN TO ROCK

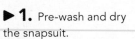 **1.** Pre-wash and dry the snapsuit.

2. Position the iron-on in the desired location on the tee. Follow the manufacturer's instructions for attaching it to the fabric.

3. Turn the snapsuit inside out when laundering.

Variation
Hammer Time

No time to appliqué? No worries. Just add a simple iron-on faux appliqué to a tee. Look for a variety of designs in craft or fabric stores.

CHAPTER 11

HOLIDAYS
& SPECIAL OCCASIONS

Holidays and special occasions provide the perfect opportunity to honor the day with a special tee or two. Best of all, since holidays are generally a busy time, you can make most of the designs in this chapter in an hour or less.

BASICS

Make Every Day a Holiday

Aside from the big holidays, special celebrations, such as weddings, birthdays, babies on board, or family reunions, are perfect for wearing a custom creation. Plus, you can purchase many craft items to make your job easier. Iron-ons, stencils, and inkjet transfers are a snap to find and easy to use.

The designs featured in this chapter are only a fraction of the ideas you can use for customizing a special-occasion tee. This is a perfect time to try out some of the techniques you learned in other chapters. Whether you celebrate Chinese New Year or Groundhog Day, have fun and let your imagination be your guide.

Q & A

Q: *Everyone else seems to come up with great design ideas. Where can I find my own?*

A: If you're stumped for design ideas, check out vintage greeting cards, wrapping paper, clip-art books, and holiday fabrics for inspiring patterns and pictures.

Wear a tee on New Year's Eve? Absolutely! With a few fancy appliqués, you'll be ready to party way past midnight.

WHEN THE CLOCK STRIKES

▶ **1.** Begin with a slinky silver tee and three premade sheer-fabric flower appliqués.

2. Sew a few small sequins and beads to each of the appliqués.

3. Position the flower appliqués along the neckline of the tee on one shoulder. Overlap them if needed. Use a needle and matching thread to hand stitch the appliqués in place.

There's nothing like tiny hands searching for colored eggs in springtime grass. A simple yet sweet design is easy to create with fabric paint, a few scraps of rickrack, and iron-on patches.

▶ **1.** Copy the template on page 174, and use it as the pattern to make your stencil on a piece of freezer paper. Use a craft knife to cut out the egg shapes.

2. Place the cut stencil wax side down on a kid's tee in the desired location. Press the paper with an iron to stick the stencil to the shirt.

3. Place a piece of wax paper inside the tee between the front and back to prevent the paint from seeping through. Paint the eggs using blue, green, and purple fabric paint. Allow the paint to dry. Peel the stencil off the shirt. Follow the manufacturer's instructions for heat setting the paint.

4. Sew scraps of rickrack or ribbon across the egg shapes.

5. Follow the manufacturer's instructions for attaching colorful daisy iron-ons to the eggs.

Valentine's Day is all about love, love, love. And nothing says it better than hearts.

LITTLE FLIRT

▶ **1.** You'll need a pink camisole and red knit fabric or an old red T-shirt you wish to recycle. If you have, or can find, a camisole printed with hearts, all the better.

2. Cut out several heart motifs from the knit fabric or recycled tee. Leave at least a 1-inch (2.5 cm) allowance around the edges. Cut lightweight, paper-backed fusible webbing to fit the heart cutouts. Follow the manufacturer's instructions for fusing the webbing to the wrong side of the fabrics.

3. Cut out the motifs by cutting away most of the allowance you left in step 2. Remove the paper backing, and place the appliqués on the camisole in the desired positions. Follow the manufacturer's instructions for fusing the appliqués to the tee.

4. Thread your machine with regular or satin thread, and use a zigzag stitch to sew around the edges of the appliqués.

5. Follow the manufacturer's instructions for attaching an iron-on word at the center of the largest heart. If desired, add extra details to the design, such as buttons, rhinestones, or bows.

● Variation
Punky Love

Use the reverse appliqué technique to sew a heart to a tee (see Chardonnay on page 73). Add a touch of punk by cutting the fabric over the appliqué into strips rather than cutting it away. Add simple ties to the sides by cutting two small holes in the tee near one side seam. Thread strips of ribbon or knit fabric through the holes, and tie them in knots.

● Variation
Love First

Mix media for stunning results. Hand gather pleats on velvet ribbon into the shape of a heart (page 13). Sew it to a floral printed shirt. Sew another layer of thinner trim or braid over the gathered velvet ribbon. Add a hand-stamped patch that reads LOVE FIRST.

It's all about red, white, and blue. If you want to create your own fireworks at the picnic, make this skirted-tee dress for your little girl, then make the variation for yourself.

▶ **1.** You'll need a girl's red tank top and a woman's tee in blue and white stripes or polka dots. Cut off the bottom of the woman's tee 9 inches (22.9 cm) up from the hem.

2. Sew a gathering stitch across the top of the piece ¾ inch (1.9 cm) in from the cut edge. Pull the threads to gather. Pin the piece to the hem of the girl's tank top, adjust the gathers, and then sew to attach. Sew a length of ribbon or rickrack over the stitching line.

3. Make the flowers and leaves using the remaining fabric from the woman's tee. First cut four simple leaf shapes. Pin two of them near the waistline and two near one strap of the tank. Sew down the center of the leaves to attach them.

4. Cut two strips from the woman's tee, each 1 inch (2.5 cm) wide and 12 inches (30.5 cm) long. Beginning at one end, fold and roll one of the strips onto itself to make a rolled flower (page 12). Use a needle and thread to sew the flower together so it will keep its shape. Make another flower using the remaining strip. Place the flowers over the leaves and sew them to the tee.

Variation
Flower Fireworks

Layering silk flowers on a lacy tank creates a fresh summer look. On one shoulder, use needle and thread to sew blue fabric-covered buttons in the center of layered red and white silk flower petals.

Thanksgiving is a time to get cozy with family and friends. Recycling a beloved worn-out sweater was the design inspiration for this fall look.

▶ **1.** You'll need a long-sleeved V-neck tee and a sweater you wish to recycle.

2. Cut off the bottom of the sweater 2 inches (5 cm) up from the hem. Sew a gathering stitch down the center of the band. Pull the threads to gather. Pin the band along the neckline of the tee from one shoulder seam to the other. Adjust the gathers and sew it in place.

3. Make the flowers. Cut the cuffs off the sweater, and then gather them into circular flower shapes. Sew the flowers to the neckline over the gathered band.

4. Stitch around the flowers to make them lie flat against the gathered band. Sew buttons to the center of each flower by hand.

● **Variation**
Falling Leaves

Use a variety of stencils to make a cascade of falling leaves on your shirt. Try stenciling with two or three colors to capture the shading of autumn leaves. You can also stencil with ivory, cream, or beige; then lightly highlight the leaves with shimmering metallic or iridescent paint.

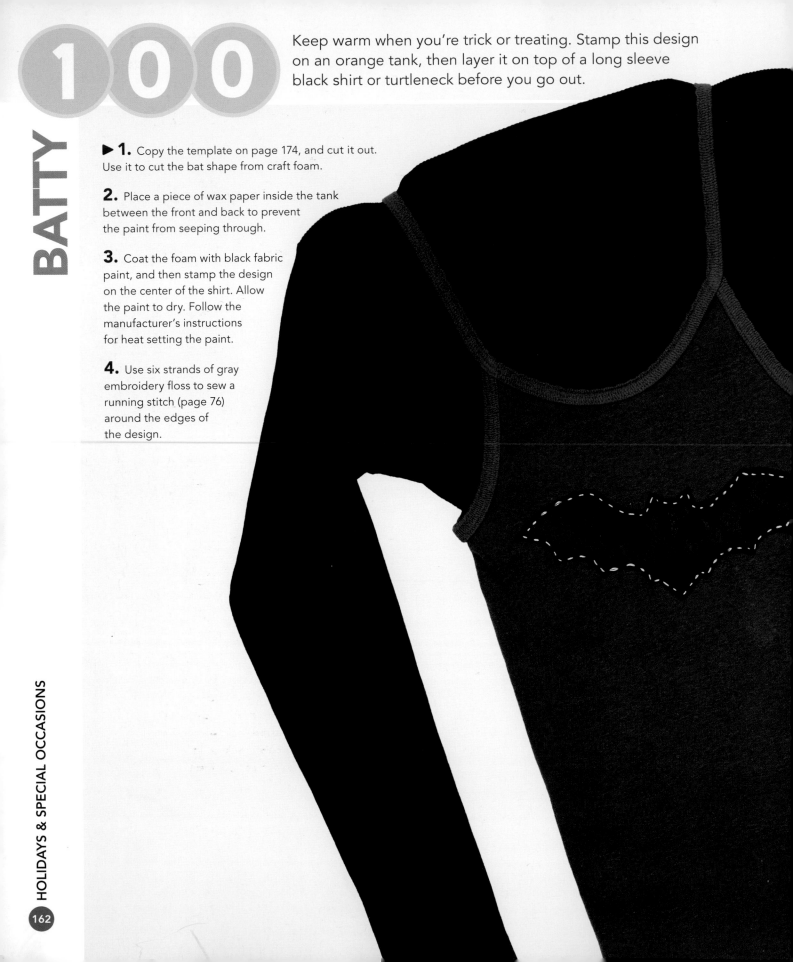

Keep warm when you're trick or treating. Stamp this design on an orange tank, then layer it on top of a long sleeve black shirt or turtleneck before you go out.

BATTY

▶ **1.** Copy the template on page 174, and cut it out. Use it to cut the bat shape from craft foam.

2. Place a piece of wax paper inside the tank between the front and back to prevent the paint from seeping through.

3. Coat the foam with black fabric paint, and then stamp the design on the center of the shirt. Allow the paint to dry. Follow the manufacturer's instructions for heat setting the paint.

4. Use six strands of gray embroidery floss to sew a running stitch (page 76) around the edges of the design.

Variation
Skully

A simple skull appliqué on a striped tee is a fun way to show off your Halloween spirit. Take a skull motif from an old tee or use the template on page 172 to make your own appliqué. You can also paint a skull on a tee using the template as your guide, or create your own design.

Show off the true holiday spirit with a custom-painted tee. Making the stencil from freezer paper will ensure crisp, sharp edges.

▶ **1.** Copy and enlarge the template on page 174 to use as the pattern for cutting your stencil. Use a craft knife to cut the stencil from a piece of freezer paper.

2. Place the cut stencil wax side down on the shirt in the desired location. Press the paper with an iron to stick the stencil to the shirt.

3. Place a piece of wax paper inside the tee between the front and back to prevent the paint from seeping through. Using black fabric paint, paint the hand and the words I'm With. Paint the word Santa in red. Allow the paint to dry. Peel the stencil off the shirt. Follow the manufacturer's instructions for heat setting the paint.

> TIP: Try designing your own sayings using a font style from your word processing program.

● **Variation**
Snowflake

White-on-white cotton prints are perfect for creating snowflake appliqués, especially when you sew them on a pastel blue tee. Use the template on page 174 as a pattern for cutting the snowflake from your fabric.

Show your solidarity with matching shirts when you go on that last single-girls' night out. Make your own designs for a fraction of the cost that bridal companies charge.

▶ **1.** Look for a premade silkscreen design that says what you want, or make your own with the words Bachelorette Party. Use fabric paint to screen the design on all shirts.

2. Use gem glue to attach rhinestones in several sizes to the design.

SOON TO BE
MRS JONES

● **Variation**
Almost Mrs.
Use iron-on letters or gems to spell out bridal sayings. Add a chunky button or rhinestone to accentuate a neckline.

BELLY BAND

▶ **1.** Measure around the hem of a tank or tee. Add 1 inch (2.5 cm) to this measurement. Cut a strip of stretchy knit fabric that is as wide as the determined measurement and 18 inches (45.7 cm) long. **Note:** Make sure the strip's width is on the stretch of the fabric.

2. Lay the fabric strip on a flat work surface. Accordion fold the 18-inch (45.7 cm) length until it measures 9 inches (22.9 cm) long. Pin the folds in place.

3. Fold the pleated fabric in half widthwise. Sew the pleated ends together using a 1-inch (2.5 cm) seam allowance.

4. Align the raw edges of the band with wrong sides together. Your band should have one pleated, sewn seam, two aligned raw edges at the top, and a soft fold opposite the raw edges.

5. Working with right sides together, position the pleated seam on the center back of a tee or tank. Align the raw edges of the band with the hem of the tee or tank, and pin. Sew the band to the tank. Trim the threads, and use pinking shears to trim any bulk from the seam.

> **TIP:** Use a ballpoint needle and slightly longer stitch to accommodate the stretch of the fabric.

Most moms-to-be aren't ready for maternity clothes in their first trimester. Adding a belly band of stretchy knit fabric to a tank or tee is a good way to take care of an early pregnancy or post-baby wardrobe.

Variation
Palm-Beach Mama

During hot summer days, moms-to-be can cool down in this cut-and-stitch design. Use scissors to remove the bottom portion of a tee just under the bust line, then sew a long cotton ruffle to the tee. Begin with two pieces of fabric that are approximately 14 inches (35.6 cm) long and twice as wide as the tee along the cut line. Note: Adjust the length of the ruffle depending on the height of the mom.

Place the pieces right sides together and sew two side seams. Hem one edge. Run a gathering stitch along the other edge. Pull the threads to gather. With right sides together, align the raw edges on the ruffle with the cut line on the tee. Adjust the gathers, and then sew the ruffle to the tee. Sew an appliqué to the ruffle. Make a 5-inch (12.7 cm) ruffle following the same directions for making the long ruffle. Overlap it on the first ruffle, wrong side to right side, and sew to attach.

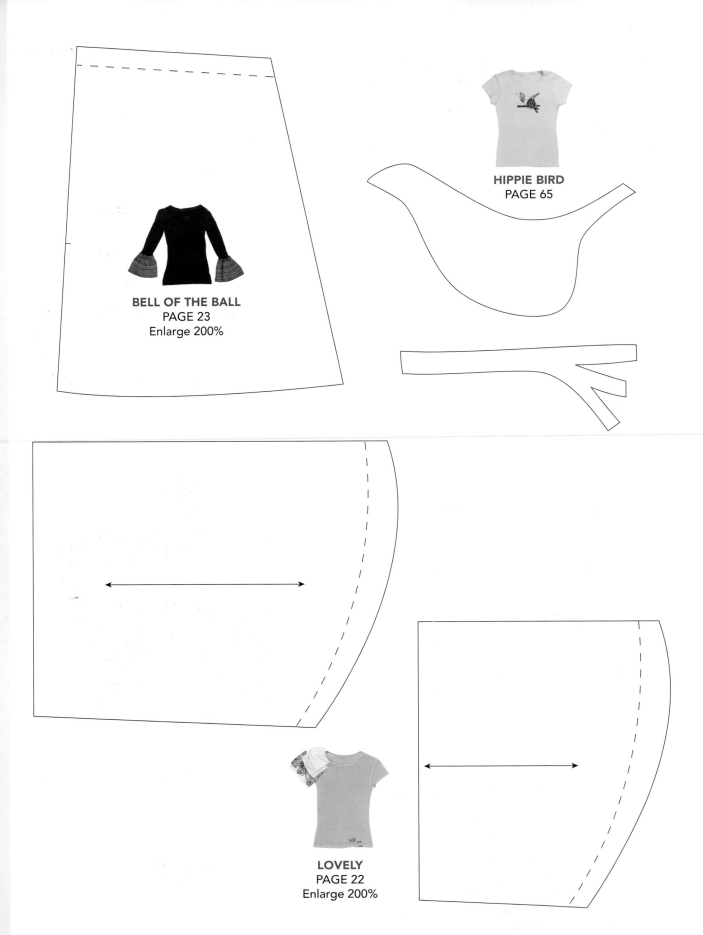

BELL OF THE BALL
PAGE 23
Enlarge 200%

HIPPIE BIRD
PAGE 65

LOVELY
PAGE 22
Enlarge 200%

MOUSTACHE

Enlarge to desired size

CITY RIDES
PAGE 32

MOUSTACHE
PAGE 33

CROWNED
PAGE 38

CITY FOREST
PAGE 64

Enlarge to desired size

FLASHBACK
PAGE 83

STRAWBERRY FIELDS
PAGE 66

CHERRY (100%)
PAGE 89

BLISS (100%)
PAGE 81

FOXY
PAGE 88

LITTLE DEAR (100%)
PAGE 86

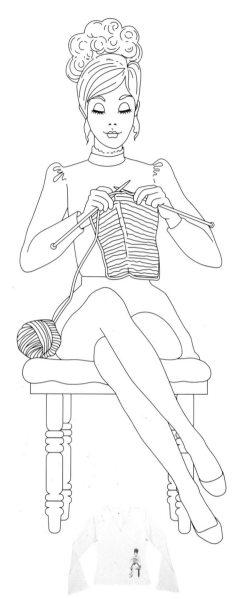

I KNIT THEREFORE I AM
PAGE 109

I ONLY HAVE EYES 4 U
PAGE 130

Enlarge to desired size

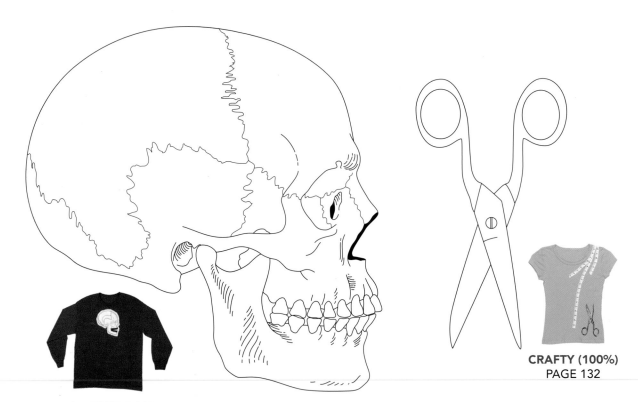

CHATTER BOX
PAGE 147

CRAFTY (100%)
PAGE 132

SKULLY
PAGE 163

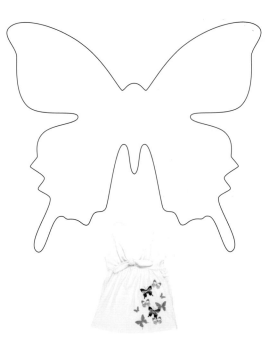

BOTANICAL (100%)
PAGE 131

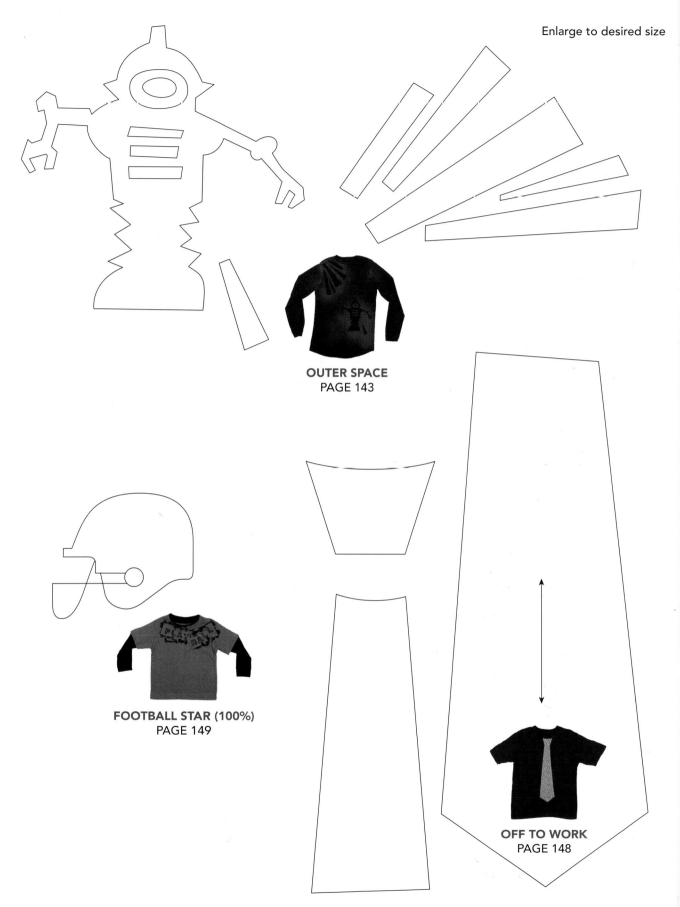

OUTER SPACE
PAGE 143

FOOTBALL STAR (100%)
PAGE 149

OFF TO WORK
PAGE 148

I'm With Santa

Enlarge to desired size

I'M WITH SANTA
PAGE 164

BATTY
PAGE 162

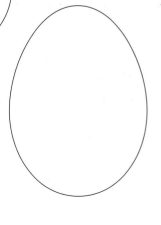

EGG DAY
PAGE 157

SNOWFLAKE
PAGE 164

About the Author

D.I.Y. guru Cathie Filian brings a fresh approach to creative living with her outside-the-box ideas for crafts, recipes, and home décor. She is a little bit country, a little bit rock-n-roll, and all original.

Cathie created, produces, and co-hosts the popular lifestyle shows *Creative Juice* and *Witch Crafts* on HGTV & DIY Network. She was nominated for an Emmy for Outstanding Lifestyle Host for her work on *Creative Juice* and for a second Emmy for Outstanding Lifestyle Host Program for her work on *Witch Crafts*.

Cathie has also appeared on numerous network shows, specials, and promos for NBC, ABC, Discovery Channel, HGTV, DIY, and Food Network. Programs such as *The Nate Berkus Show*, *Rachael Ray*, *IVillage Live*, *View From the Bay* and *The Florence Henderson Show* have featured Cathie as a "lifestyle expert."

Her first book, *Creative Juice: 45 Re-Crafting Projects*, is filled with fun and funky recycling craft ideas that can be made for pennies. Her second book, *Bow Wow WOW! Fetching Costumes for Your Fabulous Dog*, is full of patterns and ideas for creating pet fashions. Cathie's most recent book, *101 Snappy Fashions: Oodles of One-Piece Designs for Babies* shows readers how to use simple techniques like embroidery and stamping to give the everyday snapsuit a cool, new designer look. All three were published by Lark Crafts.

In addition to books, Cathie writes "Home Hobbies", a syndicated newspaper column for United Features and a Lifestyle Blog. She also contributes to national shelter publications such as *Better Homes and Gardens*, *Life* magazine, *Real Simple*, *Redbook*, and many others.

Cathie's invention, Hot Glue Gun Helpers, a line of tools for working with hot glue, helps prevent burns and allow for more creative uses with hot glue.

Cathie grew up in the Midwest and has been getting crafty for as long as she can remember. She began sewing when she was eight and her love of stitching followed her all the way to college, where she studied Textile Science and Fashion Design at Ohio State University. In her senior year she was awarded the Outstanding Senior Design Award.

Before *Creative Juice*, Cathie worked in the film business creating costumes for such films as *Rushmore*, *Twister*, *Heartbreakers*, and *Vanilla Sky*. Cathie lives in Los Angeles with her husband, Eddie, and their dog, Max.

Visit her blog (**www.cathiefilian.com**) and website (**www.cathieandsteve.com**).

Special Thanks

Thank you to all the people who made this book possible. I am thankful for all the talented people at Lark Books and for the amazing editorial and design team. You guys are the best! To Linda Kopp, Kristi Pfeffer, Jane LaFerla, and Steve Mann, thank you for the beautiful handling of this book and your creative input.

Thank you to my husband, Eddie Filian, for putting up with all the scraps of fabric that fell to the floor, glitter paint that stuck to the table, and all the trips to get more tees to alter. To my partner in crafty crime, Steve Piacenza, and to my sister, Erin Berich, thanks for looking at each T-shirt design with me. Big hugs and kisses to all my family and friends. I thank you for all your support, love, and creative energy you bring me.

INDEX

It's all on www.larkcrafts.com

Daily blog posts featuring needlearts, jewelry and beading, and all things crafty

Free, downloadable **projects** and **how-to videos**

Calls for artists and **book submissions**

A free **e-newsletter** announcing new and exciting books

...and a place to celebrate the **creative spirit**